THE FRUGAL FOODIE COOKBOOK

200 Gourmet Recipes for Any Budget

ALANNA KAUFMAN AND ALEX SMALL

Avon, Massachusetts

Published by
Adams Media, a division of F+W Media, Inc.
57 Littlefield Street, Avon, MA 02322. U.S.A.
www.adamsmedia.com

ISBN 10: 1-60550-681-8
ISBN 13: 978-1-60550-681-4

Printed in the United States of America.

J I H G F E D C B A

Library of Congress Cataloging-in-Publication Data
is available from the publisher.

This publication is designed to provide accurate and authoritative information
with regard to the subject matter covered. It is sold with the understanding
that the publisher is not engaged in rendering legal, accounting, or other
professional advice. If legal advice or other expert assistance is required, the
services of a competent professional person should be sought.
—From a *Declaration of Principles* jointly adopted by a Committee of the
American Bar Association and a Committee of Publishers and Associations

Many of the designations used by manufacturers and sellers to distinguish
their product are claimed as trademarks. Where those designations appear in
this book and Adams Media was aware of a trademark claim, the designations have been printed with initial capital letters.

This book is available at quantity discounts for bulk purchases.
For information, please call 1-800-289-0963.

For our parents.

table of
contents

part i: small dishes

APPETIZERS AND SNACKS . . . 1

SALADS . . . 15

SOUPS . . . 33

part ii: big dishes

part iii: desserts

Introduction

I'm living proof that anyone can learn to cook cost-conscious, delicious food, mostly because I am such an unlikely person to have developed this skill.

I left my parent's kitchen for college with the usual tricks—brownies from a mix and fruit-and-nut salad when I felt particularly culinary. Then I met Alex through our college newspaper, and his ease in the kitchen astounded me. On our first date, he arrived at my apartment with two armfuls of groceries, and I gaped as he casually unpacked his ingredients and began to prepare dinner. That night, he wooed me with a pear and Gorgonzola salad, followed by tender, flaky salmon fillets that he topped with a colorful homemade salsa. For dessert, he impressed me with bananas flambé over ice cream.

The meal was unlike anything I'd ever seen prepared with such limited resources. At the time, I imagined that the dishes Alex cooked would take all day to prepare and cost an unreasonable amount of money. But Alex pulled everything together in an hour, and on the budget of an ordinary college student. He floored me with contemporary recipes and meals with cohesive, delectable flavors. He prepared dishes that I wanted to eat and that tasted really good. I'll admit that I had a crush on Alex before, but after this meal, I was smitten. Who is this boy, I remember thinking, and how can I get him to cook for me every night?

Over the next few weeks, Alex introduced my small, unequipped kitchen to high-quality, contemporary flavors that I thought were impossible to achieve on my budget. I decided that I would learn to cook the foods I love to eat, and that Alex would teach me.

Luckily, he didn't seem to mind. With my limited equipment and funds, I learned to roast a chicken, mix vinaigrettes, and even make pasta from scratch. Propelled by my newfound enthusiasm, Alex and I began cooking frequently. We discovered that we could save an amazing amount of time and money by making large batches of stews and soups to freeze for another day. And when our freezers overflowed with leftovers, we began inviting our friends over for meals.

At first, we planned our menus far in advance and invited friends for chili on a Saturday night or scones for Sunday brunch. Soon, it was understood that we'd always be cooking, and that anyone was welcome to join us. Unsurprisingly, we found that our friends also found cooking to be an exciting and cost-effective alternative to eating out every night. And when we started writing about our meals on our blog, Two Fat Als, we realized that we weren't the only foodies trying out high-quality, contemporary cooking with limited resources. As we shared our recipes online, our readers responded by saying that they shared our passion for good cooking and our belief that gourmet food can exist without extravagant spending.

We're thrilled to present our cookbook because we know that fancy equipment and high costs are not necessary to create delicious food. The recipes in this book are contemporary and tasty, but anyone can execute them on a limited budget. We hope that these recipes will facilitate many happy kitchen memories and inspire you to have as much fun cooking as Alex and I have.

Alanna

Living like a Frugal Foodie

Ten Frugal Foodie Tips

There are infinite ways to save money in the kitchen, but these are some of our most effective methods. In addition to the following, we try to abide by basic cost-saving techniques like reinventing leftovers into new dishes, building meals around sale items, and buying in bulk whenever possible.

1. Use the leftovers from baked chicken to make chicken stock and freeze the stock for later (see our recipe for leftover chicken stock). Since we spend a few hours making stock every time we polish off a roasted chicken, we always have chicken stock available for soups, risottos, and other dishes. Homemade stock tastes fresher than store-bought varieties, and it saves plenty of money and time.

2. Purchase different grades of ingredients. We like to keep both a cheap and a favorite version of common ingredients like balsamic vinegar, olive oil, or mustard. We use the cheap versions for cooking and the other versions for drizzling, vinaigrettes, or when the flavor features more prominently.

3. Make frugal and filling dips for parties. When hosting dinner parties, we'll encourage our guests to fill up on frugal appetizers like hummus so that we don't need to purchase large quantities of expensive proteins.

4. Bake bread. Bread is extremely inexpensive to bake, and having a toasty slice on hand can transform any small soup or salad into a filling meal. Additionally, there are tons of uses for leftovers, such as croutons, homemade bread crumbs, or bread pudding.

5. Multiple-stop shop. We rarely buy all of our ingredients at the same location. We have different stores for produce, canned goods, meats, and fishes. And

if we don't know which store or market has the lowest price for an ingredient, we'll often split up and call each other to compare.

6. Make substitutions. This may seem obvious, but substitutions are not only a great way to save money, they're also a way to begin experimenting and cooking without recipes. You can almost always substitute cheaper cheeses, nuts, and fishes for costlier versions.

7. Use expensive ingredients wisely. There's nothing wrong with using pine nuts or expensive cheeses, but we like to incorporate them as accents to a dish, rather than featuring them as the main ingredient.

8. Freeze herbs. Because you can only buy them in premeasured amounts, it's easy to use half of a bunch of herbs and accidentally let the other half rot in the refrigerator. To avoid this fate, mince any leftover herbs, mix them with a drop of water, and pour them into ice cube trays for freezing. We pop them out whenever they're called for next.

9. Remember that dinner parties aren't the only food parties. When we want to invite friends over for food but feel daunted by footing the bill, we'll choose to host a less expensive meal like breakfast or brunch. A formal brunch party can be just as entertaining as a formal dinner party, and French toast and eggs tend to cost much less than a rib roast.

10. Keep separate cooking wine. There's no reason to break open a $20 bottle of wine when most of the alcohol will be cooked off. We scope liquor stores for cheap wine sales and keep the bottles in a separate area so that we know they are for cooking.

Top Ingredients for the Frugal Foodie Pantry

These are items that we think every frugal foodie should keep in the kitchen. Buying small amounts during every trip to the grocery store will cost more than buying large amounts when these items go on sale, so make big purchases when you spot good prices. Since most of these ingredients keep for a while, there's no need to worry about them expiring.

1. Olive oil
2. Balsamic vinegar
3. Kosher salt and freshly ground pepper
4. Rice and pasta
5. Onions and garlic
6. Sugar
7. Flour
8. Soy sauce
9. Nuts and dried fruits
10. Honey

PART I: SMALL DISHES

APPETIZERS AND SNACKS

Sweet and Savory Hot Stuffed Peppers

price $15   servings 8   price per serving $1.90

These are a sleeper hit at any party; other appetizers will get the cold shoulder as your guests pop these like candy and finish them in a blink. They're small in size, but burst with a bold, spicy flavor that's smoking hot yet refined. If pressed for time, make the paste in advance and refrigerate it for up to three hours before stuffing and baking the peppers.

1 large (32-ounce) jar whole hot vinegar peppers, vinegar reserved
1 can anchovies in oil
⅓ cup seasoned bread crumbs
¼ cup pine nuts
⅓ cup white raisins
¼ teaspoon garlic powder
2 tablespoons olive oil

Preheat oven to 350°F. Cut tops off large peppers; remove seeds. Mash anchovies with a fork; mix well with bread crumbs, nuts, raisins, and garlic powder. Drizzle in olive oil; mix to make a paste. Stuff bread mixture in peppers; place in baking dish. Put 1 cup of reserved vinegar in bottom of pan; cover with aluminum foil and bake 1 hour. Remove foil; brown 15 more minutes.

Chicken Satay

price $32   servings 8   price per serving $4

*I*t's a great accomplishment to recreate a classic restaurant dish, and this recipe makes it extremely easy to churn out a favorite Thai appetizer at home. We use chicken breasts because they are lower in fat, but you can substitute thighs and the dish will turn out more moist. If you have leftover dipping sauce, this creamy peanut spread is stellar on sandwiches or for dipping raw vegetables.

¼ cup lemongrass, minced
1 small onion, quartered
2 tablespoons grated ginger
½ teaspoon turmeric
2 tablespoons ground coriander
2 teaspoons cumin
3 tablespoons soy sauce
5 tablespoons brown sugar
1 tablespoon lime juice
6 chicken breasts
Wooden skewers (about 32)

DIPPING SAUCE:
½ cup peanut butter
½ cup coconut milk
6 tablespoons lime juice
3 tablespoons soy sauce
3 tablespoons water
1 tablespoon red curry paste
1 tablespoon grated ginger
3 cloves garlic, crushed
½ cup cilantro, chopped

For marinade, combine lemongrass, onion, ginger, turmeric, coriander, cumin, soy sauce, brown sugar, and lime juice; pulse in food processor or mix thoroughly. Cut chicken lengthwise into 2" strips. Pour marinade over chicken; let rest 1–10 hours in the refrigerator. Soak skewers in water. Preheat grill; skewer chicken. Grill 5–6 minutes on each side over medium heat, until cooked. To make dipping sauce, mix together peanut butter and coconut milk. Add remaining ingredients; stir until combined. Serve chicken with dipping sauce on side.

Fig and Fontina Flatbread

price $10   servings 5   price per serving $2

While you can serve this like a pizza, we prefer to cut it into bite-sized squares to set out before a party. This dish captures the beloved combination of fruit and cheese, and serving it on flatbread lends the dish a laid-back, Mediterranean feel. You can also serve it for dinner with a side salad or alone for lunch.

3 cups all-purpose flour, more as needed
2 teaspoons instant yeast
2 tablespoons olive oil, plus a little more
2 teaspoons coarse Kosher salt or sea salt
1 cup water
1 cup shredded Fontina cheese
1 cup shredded Parmesan cheese (Gorgonzola works, too)
½ pound dried black mission figs halved
  (or any other type of fig)

Preheat oven to 400°F. Combine flour, yeast, oil, and salt in food processor; process. Add water through feed tube; process about 30 seconds, adding more water if necessary until mixture forms a slightly sticky ball. Turn dough onto floured work surface; knead to form a smooth, round ball. Place ball in bowl; cover with plastic wrap. Let rise until double in size, 1–2 hours. Divide in ½; roll each ball flat and place on baking sheet. Rub a little olive oil over top; sprinkle on cheese and figs. Bake 8–10 minutes, until golden. Cut into squares and serve.

Pomegranate Fig Bites

price $12   servings 8   price per serving $1.50

*S*ometimes recipes develop out of necessity, and this is one of them. We had some figs and pomegranate juice in the kitchen, and people coming over for dinner. Alex threw the ingredients into a pot, and thirty minutes later he'd invented this tangy, delicious spread that our guests devoured. We later went back to recreate and record the spread, which we love to complement with creamy blue cheese and crisp wheat crackers.

12 dried figs, chopped
1 cup red wine
½ cup pomegranate juice or grape juice
3 lemon slices
2 tablespoons honey
20 wheat crackers
4 ounces blue cheese, sliced into very thin pieces

Combine figs, wine, juice, lemon slices, and honey in saucepan. Bring to a boil; turn down heat and simmer 15 minutes, until only a bit of liquid remains. Remove from heat; remove lemon slices and let cool. Spoon into a food processor or blender; pulse until smooth. Spread over crackers and top with miniature slices of blue cheese.

Grilled Peach and Shrimp Crostini

price $16   servings 8   price per serving $2

Serve this dish during the summer when the grill is going, peaches are in season, and everyone's in the mood for bold and refreshing flavors. The sharp lime vinaigrette balances the sweet summer fruit, and serving the mixture over toasted bread lends the perfect crunch. If you want to make a little extra, this bright shrimp salad also goes well over crispy greens or in a sandwich the next day.

3 peaches, halved with pits removed

1 pound shrimp, peeled and deveined

¼ cup honey

2 tablespoons Dijon mustard

Juice of 3 limes

2 tablespoons mayonnaise

Salt and pepper to taste

1 baguette (or similar amount of other bread), sliced into small pieces and toasted

Preheat grill to high. Place peach halves on grill; cook them about 3 minutes each side, until just softened. Remove, then place shrimp on grill; cook about 2 minutes each side, until cooked through. Chop shrimp and peaches into ½" cubes; place in a bowl. Whisk together honey, mustard, lime juice, mayonnaise, salt, and pepper. Adjust seasonings, then pour over shrimp and peaches; gently stir to coat. Arrange toasted bread on a platter; spoon mixture onto bread and serve.

Gourmet Chips with Smoked Salmon

price $10   servings 6   price per serving $1.65

Although smoked salmon tends to show up only during brunch hours, we're such fans of it that we're on a mission to incorporate it into other mealtimes. In this easy appetizer, we layer bits of smoked salmon onto homemade potato crisps with a dab of lemony cream. Potato crisps and smoked salmon alone are irresistible, so you can imagine how tempting the results are when their flavors combine.

10 fingerling potatoes, sliced into ⅛" rounds
1 tablespoon olive oil
Salt and pepper to taste
2 tablespoons chives, chopped
1 tablespoon horseradish
½ cup sour cream
1 tablespoon lemon juice
2 slices smoked salmon, cut into 1" pieces

Preheat oven to 350°F. Toss potatoes in olive oil and season generously with salt and pepper. Roast for about 20–30 minutes, flipping once, until very crispy. Let potatoes cool. Mix together chives, horseradish, sour cream, and lemon juice. Spoon a small amount of sour cream mixture on each potato chip and top with a small piece of smoked salmon.

Onion-Parmesan Crisps

This is one of the easiest appetizers in our repertoire—ideal for an impromptu dinner party when there's no time to run to the grocery store or a simple snack for the family. Not only does it use ingredients you probably have at home, it's extremely quick to make.

3 tablespoons low-fat mayonnaise   2 tablespoons grated Parmesan cheese

3 thin slices red onion, chopped   12 Melba crackers

In a small bowl, combine mayonnaise, onion, and Parmesan. Spread mixture on crackers; place on a baking sheet. Broil in oven 5 minutes, until topping is golden brown, then serve.

Avocado Boats

Our love for avocado is borderline obsessive, and we've found that we aren't the only ones. We often invent sandwiches or salads just to sneak in a few slices, but in this dish the devotion to avocado is anything but clandestine. So if you, like us, love avocado, here's a legitimate excuse to eat it unabashedly (as if you needed one).

½ cup French dressing   Juice of ½ lemon

3 tablespoons low-fat mayonnaise   Salt and pepper to taste

2 teaspoons anchovy paste   2 ripe Haas avocados, halved with pits removed

In a small bowl, combine French dressing, mayonnaise, anchovy paste, and lemon juice. Use whisk to mix ingredients; season with salt and pepper. Arrange each avocado half on a plate. Fill cavity of each avocado with anchovy mixture and serve.

Cucumber Tea Sandwiches

price $6   servings 6   price per serving $1

*T*hese sandwiches are refreshing and light for summer. Each bite is luxurious, as the cool crunch of cucumbers melts into whipped cream cheese and soft baguette. Inexpensive decadence, indeed.

1 large cucumber, halved lengthwise
4–6 ounces whipped cream cheese
½ whole-wheat baguette, sliced into 12 (½") rounds
Salt and pepper to taste
Flat-leaf parsley (for garnish)

Using a peeler, peel the flat side of cucumber to form long, thin ribbons; set ribbons aside. Spread a thin layer of cream cheese over bread slices; gently place cucumber slices on each slice of bread. Reserve any extra cucumber for sandwiches or salad later. Turn bread over; use a sharp knife to cut around edge to remove excess cucumber. Carefully turn bread slices cucumber-side up; sprinkle with salt and pepper. Garnish with parsley and serve.

Sausage-Stuffed Mushrooms

price $15   servings 10   price per serving $1.50

*S*tuffed mushrooms tend to be crowd pleasers, and these are no exception. They're spicy and moist, with pretty green peppers to add a spot of color.

50 large white button mushrooms
½ large onion, finely chopped
½ green pepper, finely chopped
3 garlic cloves, minced
3 tablespoons olive oil
⅓ pound spicy Italian sausage, cooked and finely chopped
⅓ cup seasoned bread crumbs
⅓ cup grated Parmesan cheese
¼–½ cup chicken broth

Wash mushrooms and scoop out stems, reserving them. Place caps right-side up on a baking sheet; set aside. Finely chop mushroom stems; combine with onion, green pepper, and garlic. Sauté in olive oil in a large skillet until soft. Remove from heat; toss with cooked sausage, bread crumbs, and cheese. Continue to cook until mixture is thick and dry. Add enough broth to moisten to consistency of stuffing. Using a spoon, stuff mushroom caps with enough mixture to mound slightly. Broil about 8 minutes, or until slightly crispy and brown on top.

Simple Steamed Mussels

price $12   servings 4   price per serving $3

*T*his is a recipe for mussels in a light but flavorful broth. While it's not quite a soup, the liquid is delicious, and we'll often finish it with spoons or mop it up with French bread after the mussels are gone.

1 cup chicken broth
½ cup white wine
3 tablespoons lemon juice
½ red onion, chopped
½ cup parsley, chopped
1 pound cleaned mussels (discard any that have opened)
Salt and pepper to taste
Sliced French bread (optional)

Put first 5 ingredients in a 4-quart pot; bring to a boil. Add mussels; steam until cooked and fully open. Discard any unopened mussels; adjust seasonings. Ladle into individual serving bowls; use bread to soak up broth.

Shrimp and Veggie Pot Stickers

price $20   servings 12   price per serving $1.65

Nothing stimulates our urge to cook like being busy. After packed work days sustained only by coffee, we rush home to create obscene amounts of comfort food. These pot stickers are perfect for the task of de-stressing: They're packed with flavor from the ginger and scallions, and methodically folding them up is one of our favorite ways to unwind.

1 pound shrimp, deveined, shelled, and chopped finely
¼ head napa cabbage, shredded
4 carrots, shredded
1 bunch scallions, finely chopped
4 (1") cubes fresh ginger, grated
¼ cup soy sauce
⅛ cup sesame oil
48 wonton wrappers

DIPPING SAUCE:
¼ cup soy sauce
¼ cup rice wine vinegar
Pinch sugar

Combine everything but wrappers in large bowl; mix thoroughly. Scoop teaspoon-sized ball of filling into middle of wrapper. Fold wrapper in half and press edges together. Fold the edge over itself again about ⅛" to create a seam. Repeat until all dumplings are formed. Steam 10 minutes; cool and serve. For dipping sauce, combine soy sauce and rice wine vinegar together with pinch of sugar to taste.

Endive with Blue Cheese Spread

price $10   servings 10   price per serving $1

It's impossible to go wrong with Gorgonzola and walnuts, so we try to incorporate the combination into as many dishes as possible. We use it for salads, sandwiches, and, here, in an appetizer that's at once smooth, crunchy, sweet, and tangy. Endive leaves are so elegant and lend a complementary crunch to this alluring spread.

1 cup Gorgonzola cheese, crumbled
¼ cup dried cranberries, chopped
¼ cup walnuts, chopped
2 tablespoons olive oil
2 tablespoons raspberry vinegar
1 tablespoon Dijon mustard
1 tablespoon honey
Salt and pepper to taste
2 heads endive

In a food processor or bowl, combine cheese, cranberries, walnuts, olive oil, vinegar, mustard, and honey. Blend until mixture forms a paste; season with salt and pepper. Separate endive leaves; arrange on a platter. Spread Gorgonzola mixture onto leaves and serve.

Tuna Tomato Halves

price $5 servings 4 price per serving $2.50

*I*n our early days cooking together, we argued over whose recipe for tuna fish salad is superior. I make mine with red wine vinegar, salt, and pepper; Alex's plays up lemon and relish. We now alternate the recipes depending on the dish. In this easy appetizer, Alex's recipe prevails because the lemony bite in his version goes beautifully with ripe summer tomatoes.

2 small vine tomatoes
1 can chunk white tuna
2 tablespoons mayonnaise
Juice of 1 lemon
¼ cup sweet gherkins pickles, thinly sliced
1 tablespoon relish
Salt and pepper to taste
4 chives, chopped into 2" pieces for garnish

Halve tomatoes; scoop out flesh so only shell remains. (It may be too wet to use, but you can try to reserve tomato innards to use later in a salad or a sandwich.) In a bowl, combine tuna, mayonnaise, lemon juice, pickles, and relish; stir until combined. Season with salt and pepper. Scoop tuna salad into tomato shells; garnish with chives and serve.

PART I: SMALL DISHES

SALADS

Blueberry and Blue Cheese Salad

price $12 servings 6 price per serving $2

This salad is monochrome: blueberries, blue cheese, and blueberry dressing. It's funny, because dressing in monochrome is among Alex's biggest fears. He hates blue shirts with blue jeans, but there's no denying his adoration of the sophisticated trio of "blues" in this salad. Make it during summertime with freshly picked blueberries, and we guarantee that the color combination will enter your weekly rotation of meals, if not wardrobe.

1 bag mixed greens
1 head romaine lettuce, cut up
3 ounces Gorgonzola cheese
2 cups blueberries
2 cups walnuts, coarsely chopped

DRESSING:
1 cup blueberries
⅔ cup olive oil
⅓ cup balsamic vinegar
Salt and pepper to taste
Sugar, as needed

Combine greens, romaine, Gorgonzola, and blueberries on a large platter. Toast walnuts at 350°F for about 3 minutes, until they are a light golden brown and aromatic, watching them to make sure they do not burn. To make dressing, pulse blueberries in food processor about 10 seconds; whisk together with oil and vinegar. Add salt and pepper. If blueberries are not very sweet, add sugar as needed. Drizzle dressing over salad and serve.

Citrus Avocado Salad

price $15   servings 6   price per serving $2.50

We don't know whether we're more seduced by the taste or the beauty of this gorgeous salad contained within an orange cup. The salad stars bright and refreshing Asian-inspired flavors, and we use an easy technique to turn orange peels into exotic bowls for a breathtaking presentation. Once you have the technique down, use the orange cups for serving fruit salad or sorbet.

3 large navel oranges
2 Hass avocados, cubed
1 bunch scallions, finely chopped
½ cup cashews, preferably unsalted

DRESSING:
1 teaspoon sesame oil
¼ cup olive oil
2 tablespoons rice wine vinegar
4 tablespoons fresh orange juice
Salt and pepper to taste

Place an orange on table with navel facing you. Insert a knife into top on diagonal; make similar inserts in zigzag formation around fruit. Separate the halves; carefully remove fruit from peel. Cut orange sections into bite-sized pieces; place in bowl. Repeat for other oranges. Add avocados and scallions; whisk together dressing ingredients and add until salad is very lightly covered. Add cashews; spoon salad back into empty orange halves. Serve.

Cranberry-Apple-Walnut Salad

price $20   servings 4   price per serving $5

This is one of our favorite salads to serve during the winter because the red cranberries and green apples are so festive and seasonal. It's also extremely easy to multiply the recipe for crowds, so it's perfect and easy for holiday potlucks and parties. Though the salad is tart on its own, the sweet dressing balances out the dish.

2 heads romaine lettuce, chopped
1 Granny Smith apple, cored and chopped into ½-inch cubes
½ cup walnuts, lightly toasted
½ cup dried cranberries
3 ounces feta cheese

DRESSING:
½ cup olive oil
3 tablespoons raspberry vinegar
1 tablespoon honey
Salt and pepper to taste

In a large salad bowl, combine lettuce, apple, walnuts, and cranberries. Crumble feta cheese over top. Whisk together olive oil, vinegar, honey, salt, and pepper; dress and toss salad just before serving.

Garden Salad with Lemon-Herb Dressing

price $8   servings 4   price per serving $2

This herb-filled dressing brings a basic garden salad up a few notches Adjust the herbs in the dressing to highlight your favorites, and feel free to add any other seasonal vegetables for a crisply fresh dish.

2 heads romaine, chopped
1 red bell pepper, thinly sliced
1 green bell pepper, thinly sliced
1 carrot, grated
1 cucumber, thinly sliced
1 tomato, sliced

DRESSING:
1 tablespoon fresh dill
1 tablespoon fresh tarragon
1 tablespoon fresh cilantro
1 tablespoon fresh parsley
1 tablespoon fresh green onion
½ cup olive oil
3 tablespoons lemon juice
1 teaspoon sugar
1 teaspoon Dijon mustard
Salt and pepper to taste

Combine salad ingredients in a large bowl. For dressing, finely chop dill, tarragon, cilantro, parsley, and green onion. Combine herbs, olive oil, lemon juice, sugar, and mustard in a small bowl. Use a whisk to mix ingredients; add salt and pepper. Dress and toss salad just before serving.

Grape and Walnut Salad

price $12   servings 4   price per serving $3

*T*his is a great salad that is both cheap and filling—no meat is needed! The creamy dressing paired with the avocados is luxuriously smooth, but the grapes and walnuts balance the salad out with a little tang and crunch.

9 ounces mixed greens
3 bunches red grapes, halved
2 cups walnuts, toasted
2 Haas avocados, cut into 1" pieces

DRESSING:
1 cup mayonnaise
1 tablespoon Worcestershire sauce
1 tablespoon lime juice
1 tablespoon yellow curry powder
⅓ cup olive oil
2 tablespoons balsamic vinegar
Salt and pepper to taste

Toss salad ingredients together in a large bowl and divide among plates. Whisk together dressing ingredients and dress each plate before serving.

Sunset Tomato Salad

price $8   servings 4   price per serving $2

No matter how excited we are for fall produce when September arrives, we always pay homage to the sweet succulence of summer vegetables with a final tomato salad. Tomatoes are beautiful and inexpensive in early fall, and it's easy to find them cheaply at the farmer's market.

2 large yellow tomatoes, chopped into 1" cubes
2 large beefsteak tomatoes, chopped into 1" cubes
¼ tablespoon olive oil
3 tablespoons balsamic vinegar
¼ cup fresh basil, chopped
½ teaspoon fresh or dried oregano
Salt and pepper to taste
12 ounces spring mix lettuce

Mix chopped tomatoes with olive oil, balsamic vinegar, basil, oregano, salt, and pepper. Divide lettuce evenly among plates and top with tomato mixture.

Peanut-Lime Mexican Medley

price $24   servings 6   price per serving $4

We love to make this salad for large group dinners because people go crazy over the unexpected combination of the two dressings. The dressings don't work independently as salad dressings, but add them separately to your salad and mix all of the ingredients together for an eye-popping explosion of the contrasting lime and peanut flavors.

2 heads romaine lettuce, thinly sliced
1 tomato, cut into ½" pieces
1 green pepper, cut into ½" pieces
1 cup canned black beans, drained
1 cup cooked corn, drained
½ cup red onion, finely chopped
½ cup Cheddar cheese, grated
3 cups tortilla chips

SESAME DRESSING:
¼ cup peanut butter
¼ cup soy sauce
¼ cup hot water
2 teaspoons sesame oil
1 teaspoon ground ginger

LIME DRESSING:
½ cup lime juice
4 teaspoons honey mustard
⅓ cup honey
¼ cup olive oil
1 garlic clove, minced
1 teaspoon pepper
½ teaspoon salt

In a large salad bowl, combine lettuce, tomato, green pepper, black beans, corn, and onion. Make salad dressings separately in individual bowls by combining ingredients with a whisk. Dress salad first with sesame dressing, followed by lime dressing. Top with cheese and serve with tortilla chips crumbled on top.

Perfect Poached-Egg Frisée Salad

price $8   servings 4   price per serving $2

Whenever we go out for brunch, Alanna is torn between the brunch and lunch menus. So if there's ever a salad available with breakfast ingredients like eggs or smoked salmon, she's sure to order it. This salad is a creation of that desire—to eat a morning dish that is not too heavy but that still features classic breakfast flavors.

3 slices French bread, cut into 1½" cubes
1 tablespoon olive oil
1 garlic clove, crushed
3 strips bacon
1 shallot, chopped
4 tablespoons plus 2 tablespoons white vinegar
1 tablespoon sugar
Salt and pepper to taste
6 cups frisée lettuce, torn into pieces
4 eggs

To make croutons, toss bread cubes with olive oil and garlic; toast lightly in a toaster oven or in the oven at 325°F for 10 minutes and set aside. Cook bacon in heavy pan until crispy, about 8 minutes; remove and drain on paper towels. When cooled, chop and set aside. Pour off all but 2 tablespoons of bacon fat in pan; add chopped shallot and 4 tablespoons vinegar to deglaze pan. Add sugar, salt, and pepper; set aside as dressing. Arrange lettuce on 4 plates with bacon and croutons. Gently boil 2 quarts water in large saucepan with 2 tablespoons vinegar; add eggs and poach 3–5 minutes, until done. Top each salad with a poached egg and dressing.

Veggie Chopped Salad

price $12   servings 4   price per serving $3

Alanna's family has a habit of eating a salad obsessively for months, then ditching it for another. Many of the salad recipes in this book are adaptations of those recipes, including this crunchy, textured vegetable symphony, which her family ate every night for a summer. Some vegetables can be substituted depending on preferences, but we recommend keeping the hearts of palm and chickpeas as staples.

2 heads romaine lettuce, chopped
1 can chickpeas, drained
1 cucumber, chopped
2 Roma tomatoes, chopped
1 can hearts of palm, chopped
1 red pepper, chopped
1 cup button mushrooms, chopped
1 Haas avocado, chopped

DRESSING:
⅓ cup balsamic vinegar
⅔ cup olive oil
2 tablespoons Dijon mustard
Salt and pepper to taste

Combine salad ingredients in a large bowl. Whisk together dressing ingredients and serve over salad.

Roasted Beet and Pistachio Salad

price $8   servings 4   price per serving $2

It's immature, but beets crack us up. Touch them once, and your fingers are pink for days. We usually have to chase each other around the kitchen with beet fingers for 5 minutes or so before we can begin cooking with them. This salad pairs the sweet juiciness of beets with salty pistachio nuts over greens with a light dressing—a combination definitely worth a week of pink fingers.

6 small beets, peeled
2 tablespoons olive oil
Salt and pepper to taste
2 cups pistachio nuts, preferably unsalted
8 cups mixed greens

DRESSING:
⅔ cup olive oil
¼ cup red wine vinegar
¼ cup balsamic vinegar
Pinch sugar
Salt and pepper to taste

Preheat oven to 425°F. Cut beets in half; place in a roasting pan tossed with 2 tablespoons olive oil, salt, and pepper. Roast about 45 minutes to 1 hour, or until soft. Meanwhile, make dressing by mixing olive oil, vinegars, sugar, salt, and pepper. Arrange pistachios on mixed greens. Slice beets and arrange on salad. Top with dressing while beets are still warm and serve.

Roasted Tomato and Asparagus Panzanella

price  $12   servings 4   price per serving $3

*T*his salad stands alone as a filling and lovely main-course dish. The hot and toasty bread soaks up the yummy flavors of the roasted vegetables, so go for a good-quality loaf if possible. This salad is especially apropos for warm weather when tomatoes are in season, and you can grill the vegetables and bread slices instead of roasting them for an even smokier flavor.

1 loaf day-old bread, cut into 1" cubes
4 tablespoons olive oil
1 garlic clove, crushed
Salt and pepper to taste
1 bunch asparagus, cut into 1" pieces
1 red pepper, cut into ½" pieces
4 ounces cherry tomatoes, halved

DRESSING:
⅓ cup olive oil
3 tablespoons red wine vinegar
1 shallot, diced
1 teaspoon Dijon mustard
Salt and pepper to taste

Preheat oven to 350°F. Toss bread cubes with 2 tablespoons olive oil, crushed garlic, salt, and pepper. Separately, toss asparagus, red pepper, and tomatoes with remaining 2 tablespoons olive oil, salt, and pepper. Arrange bread cubes and vegetables on 2 separate baking trays; roast 15–20 minutes, until bread is crisp and vegetables are slightly softened. Whisk together dressing ingredients. Combine all ingredients in a large salad bowl; toss with dressing. Serve immediately.

Balsamic-Dressed Roasted Veggie Salad

price $30   servings 5   price per serving $6

This is among Alanna's favorite meals. When it's her turn to pick a meal for her birthday or an occasion, this is more than likely to appear on the menu. The beauty of the salad stems from two sources: its flexibility and its dressing. It doesn't matter if you use the vegetables we recommend or any others you can imagine. Throw in whatever veggies you have, and as long as you make the reduced balsamic vinaigrette, this is sure to stun.

1 zucchini, sliced lengthwise into ½" pieces

1 yellow summer squash, sliced lengthwise into ½" pieces

1 bunch asparagus

1 large portobello mushroom, sliced lengthwise into ½" pieces

1 pepper, quartered

1 eggplant, sliced into ½" thick rounds

2 tablespoons olive oil

Salt and pepper to taste

1 head romaine lettuce, chopped

1 head radicchio, chopped

1 cup cooked corn, preferably roasted

1 tomato, chopped

DRESSING:

1 cup balsamic vinegar

2 teaspoons sugar

⅔ cup olive oil

Salt and pepper to taste

Preheat oven to 350°F. Toss zucchini, squash, asparagus, mushroom, pepper, and eggplant with 2 tablespoons olive oil to coat; add salt and pepper. Place in a baking dish; cook about 30–40 minutes, until vegetables are tender. Set aside to cool; cut all vegetables into ½" pieces and combine with other salad ingredients in large bowl. To make dressing, bring vinegar to a boil in a small saucepan; simmer until vinegar has reduced to ⅓ cup. Remove from heat; stir in sugar. Cool, whisk in olive oil, and add salt and pepper. Arrange salads on plates, drizzle dressing on top, and serve.

Summer Salad with Basil-Mint Dressing

price $15   servings 6   price per serving  $2.50

Strawberries, grapes, and oranges rarely headline a green salad, but they go incredibly well with this sweet and savory basil dressing. The salad is unusual but delicious, and requires almost no preparation.

1 cup grapes, halved
1½ cups strawberries, chopped
2 oranges, sectioned and cut into 1" pieces
2 heads romaine lettuce, cut into pieces

DRESSING:
½ cup packed fresh basil leaves
½ cup packed fresh mint leaves
¼ teaspoon orange zest, grated
¼ cup fresh orange juice
2 teaspoons balsamic vinegar
1 garlic clove, chopped
½ cup olive oil

Combine salad ingredients and place a handful on each plate. Put all dressing ingredients in blender; blend until emulsified. Pour over salad.

Radish-Cucumber-Beet Salad

price $12   servings 4   price per serving $3

Our take on the beautiful yet bitter radish is simple and classy: toss it with other crunchy vegetables and dress with vinaigrette to create a flavorful, healthy summer salad. We serve this salad over romaine lettuce as a main course, but it makes a pretty first-course salad without romaine.

1 bunch beets, halved

Salt and pepper to taste

⅔ cups plus 2 tablespoons olive oil

1 cucumber, thinly sliced

½ red onion, thinly sliced

1 bunch radishes, thinly sliced

2 tablespoons fresh mint, chopped

2 tablespoons red wine vinegar

1 head romaine lettuce, chopped

Preheat oven to 375°F. Place beets in a roasting pan; sprinkle with salt, pepper, and 2 tablespoons olive oil. Roast until beets are easily pierced with a knife, about 1 hour. Let cool, then peel off skins and slice into ¼" pieces. Place cucumber in bowl; add onions and radishes. Mix together mint, olive oil, and vinegar, then add to cucumber and radish mixture. Divide lettuce among 4 plates; top with beets, then cucumber and radish mixture.

Classic Chicken Caesar

price $15   servings 5   price per serving $3

No one we know will attempt a Caesar salad when we're around because it's understood that no recipe will surpass this one. We make it frequently for dinner, but also bring it to picnics and serve it as an appetizer for dinner parties. It's a classic recipe, distinguished by its signature lemony dressing and a perfect lettuce-to-dressing ratio. As far as we've tasted, there's no better recipe out there.

DRESSING:
2 garlic cloves
2 tablespoons kosher salt
3 tablespoons mayonnaise
Juice of 3 lemons, divided
Worcestershire sauce
Salt and pepper to taste

2 chicken breasts
2 tablespoons olive oil
1 lemon
1 clove garlic, crushed
2 heads romaine lettuce, chopped
Parmesan cheese, freshly grated

CROUTONS:
1 French baguette, cut into 1" cubes
2 tablespoons olive oil
1 clove garlic, crushed
Salt to taste

In a large wooden salad bowl, crush 2 garlic cloves into salt; rub around bowl. Discard garlic. In the same bowl, whisk together mayonnaise and juice of 2 lemons; add a few dashes of Worcestershire sauce and season with salt and pepper. In a separate bowl, toss chicken with olive oil, juice of 1 lemon, garlic, salt, and pepper. On outdoor grill or under broiler, cook chicken 4–5 minutes on each side, until cooked through. Let rest 5 minutes; slice thinly. To make croutons, toss bread with olive oil, garlic, and salt; bake on baking sheet in 325°F oven 20 minutes. Toss dressing with lettuce and sprinkle with cheese. Add chicken and croutons before serving.

Vietnamese Chicken and Mint Salad

price $24   servings 8   price per serving $3

This is the salad that launched our obsession with Asian-inspired salads. And although we experimented with many salads during that time, this one remains our favorite. It requires a good amount of chopping, but it's worth the amazing combination of sweetness, tang, and crunch that results. If you can, save some in the refrigerator for the next day—the flavors meld together even more delectably over time.

1 chili pepper, minced
2 garlic cloves, minced
1 tablespoon sugar
1½ teaspoons rice wine vinegar
1½ tablespoons lime juice
1½ tablespoons fish sauce
1½ tablespoons vegetable oil
¼ medium onion, thinly sliced
1 teaspoon black pepper
½ head cabbage, shredded
1 medium carrot, cut into thin strips
2 cooked chicken breasts, cut into thin strips or shredded
Bunch of fresh mint, plus more for garnish
Salt to taste

In a bowl, combine chili pepper, garlic, sugar, vinegar, lime juice, fish sauce, oil, onion, and black pepper. In a large bowl, mix cabbage, carrot, chicken, and mint. Pour dressing over cabbage mixture; toss well. Add salt; let sit in the refrigerator for least 15 minutes before serving cold.

Winter Blood Orange Salad

price $12   servings 4   price per serving $3

When we make salad as a main course, we feel pressure to weigh it down with nuts, cheese, and other proteins to make sure it is filling enough. While we love dinner salads, there is still something to be said for just lettuce, avocado, and blood oranges. Add a simple citrus dressing and enjoy the combination of these three ingredients.

DRESSING:
½ cup olive oil
⅓ cup lemon juice
1 tablespoon sugar
1 small shallot, diced
Salt and pepper to taste

2 cups mixed greens
1 Haas avocado, sliced
1 blood orange, sectioned

Mix dressing ingredients in a small bowl; whisk until combined. Arrange lettuce, avocado, and blood oranges on a plate and add dressing.

PART I: SMALL DISHES
SOUPS

Mixed Mushroom Soup

price $6   servings 4   price per serving $1.50

*I*t's impossible to imagine a soup simpler than this one. It's extremely healthy and comes together in less than 30 minutes. You can use frozen mushrooms from a bag, so keep some handy and you'll be able to make the soup anytime.

1 onion, finely chopped
2 tablespoons olive oil
10 ounces mixed mushrooms
½ teaspoon fresh thyme
2 cups chicken stock
Salt and pepper to taste
½ cup milk or cream (optional)

In a medium saucepan, sauté onions in olive oil until soft. Add mushrooms and thyme; continue to cook until mushrooms soften. Add 1 cup of stock; cook 5 minutes. Let soup cool slightly, then add soup to blender; blend until smooth. Add additional stock to blender until desired consistency is reached. Season generously with salt and pepper. Add milk or cream, if desired, for a creamy consistency.

Bok Choy Soup

price $16   servings 4   price per serving $4

We haven't figured out why, but Mondays are often Asian soup nights for us. We love ordering noodle soups at restaurants and began to experiment with our own versions at home, throwing in different vegetables and proteins. This is one of our favorites, as the bok choy lends the broth a subtle but delicious twist, and the poached chicken adds protein for a satisfying one-dish meal.

3 scallions (plus 1 additional for poaching chicken)

1 tablespoon minced ginger (plus 1" piece sliced, for poaching chicken)

2 teaspoons soy sauce (plus 1 additional for poaching chicken)

2 chicken breasts, poached and sliced

4 cups chicken stock

2 tablespoons rice vinegar

2 tablespoons mirin (Japanese sweet rice wine)

2 cups shitake mushrooms, sliced

6 baby bok choy, cut into ½" pieces

To poach chicken, add 1 scallion 1" piece ginger, and 1 tablespoon soy sauce to a medium saucepan filled with water; bring to a boil. Add chicken; turn off heat. Cover tightly and let sit 45–55 minutes (depending on size of chicken breasts), until chicken is cooked through. Remove and let cool; slice into strips and set aside. In a large pot, combine stock, soy sauce, rice vinegar, mirin, and ginger; bring to a boil. Add mushrooms; reduce heat and simmer 5 minutes. Add bok choy, scallions, and chicken; cook 3–5 minutes, until bok choy is soft. Adjust seasonings if necessary, spoon into bowls, and serve.

Butternut Squash and Apple Soup

price $18   servings 12   price per serving $1.50

*T*his soup tastes like the cool crispness and snug coziness of fall swirled into a bowl of velvety goodness. The apples lend the soup a bright, sweet flavor, the texture is soft, and the color is sunny and warm. Plus, the little apple strips add a delicate and gorgeous garnish guests will love at an autumn dinner party.

3 tablespoons olive oil

2 onions, finely chopped

3 pounds butternut squash, peeled and chopped into 2" pieces

4 Gala apples, peeled and chopped into 2" pieces

1 teaspoon cinnamon

6 cups chicken stock

½ teaspoon nutmeg

1½ cups apple cider

Salt and pepper to taste

1 Granny Smith apple, cut into very thin strips (for garnish)

Heat olive oil in a large pot; add onions and sauté until soft and slightly browned. Add squash, Gala apples, cinnamon, and nutmeg; cook, stirring frequently, about 15 minutes. Add apple cider and chicken stock; bring to a boil 3 minutes. Reduce heat to medium; cook, partially covered, until squash is soft, about 30 minutes. Cool slightly, and transfer batches of soup to blender; blend until smooth. Return everything to pot; season with salt and pepper. Pour into bowls and garnish with a few slices of Granny Smith apples.

Creamless Broccoli Soup

price $10   servings 4   price per serving $2.50

Growing up, we loved soup with huge chunks of broccoli swimming in milky, cheesy broth. Although we can't tolerate soup with that much dairy anymore, we sometimes crave it anyway. As a result, we devised this recipe to recreate the smoothness of creamy broccoli soup without adding cream. The potatoes keep it thick and smooth, and the result is a soup that satisfies our cravings without any side effects.

3 tablespoons olive oil

1 cup onion

4 small potatoes, cut into chunks

2 leeks, sliced

1 carrot, sliced

3 tablespoons mustard seed

1½ pounds broccoli, cut into florets

5 cups chicken stock

Juice of 1 lemon

Salt and pepper to taste

Parmesan cheese or sour cream for garnish (optional)

Heat oil in a large pot. Add onion, potatoes, leeks, carrot, and mustard seed; cook 5–7 minutes. Add broccoli and stock; simmer 20 minutes, or until vegetables are soft. Cool slightly, then working in batches, blend in blender until smooth. Return to pot, and add lemon juice, salt, and pepper. Garnish with Parmesan cheese or sour cream, if desired, and serve.

Spicy Black Bean Soup

price $12   servings 6   price per serving $2

This ranks among our most delicious and favorite go-to recipes for any occasion. Not only is it extremely inexpensive and easy, the ingredients meld lusciously into a bold soup that's overflowing with spicy Latin flavors. The soup is so thick and textured that you can even scoop it up with chips or carrots. Make a vegan version by substituting vegetable broth for beef broth.

4 carrots, diced
2 medium onions, diced
1 garlic clove, chopped
2 tablespoons olive oil
1 tablespoon ground cumin
¼ teaspoon cayenne
1 teaspoon ground coriander
4 cups beef broth
½ cup long-grain rice
2 (16-ounce) cans black beans with liquid
¼ cup sherry (or substitute cooking sherry for a more frugal option)
Salt and pepper to taste

In a large stockpot, cook carrots, onions, and garlic in oil over moderate heat until softened, about 3 minutes. Stir in cumin, cayenne, and coriander; cook 1 minute. Add broth, rice, and beans; bring to a boil and then simmer 20 minutes, or until rice is soft. Cool slightly, then using a blender, purée half of mixture; return to pot. Stir in sherry and salt and pepper.

Get-Well Soup

price $8   servings 8   price per serving $1

When everyone we know gets sick in the fall, we make a huge pot of this soup and invite all of them over for some much-needed nourishment. Those who make it over usually feel better after a bowl or two. We're partial to the cute shape of pastina, but substitute whatever pasta shape makes you feel happiest.

1 whole chicken, cut into parts
1 large potato, quartered and peeled
2 medium onions, quartered
2 carrots, cut into chunks
2 stalks celery with greens, quartered
1 bunch fresh flat-leaf parsley
1 14-ounce can stewed tomatoes
1 tablespoon tomato paste
2 teaspoons salt
Salt and pepper to taste
1 pound pastina, or other small pasta

Place chicken, vegetables, and tomato paste in large stock pot; fill pot with water. Add 2 teaspoons salt; cook over high heat. Bring to boil, then reduce heat to low. Cover and cook 2 hours. Use slotted spoon to remove large chicken and vegetable pieces; pour remaining soup through strainer back into the pot. Adjust seasonings with salt and pepper. In another pot, boil water to cook pastina according to package instructions. If you like, cut up potato, carrot, or other cooked vegetables to add back into soup. Spoon broth into bowls, add pastina and cut up vegetables, and serve hot. Add slices of the chicken back into the soup, or reserve for a chicken salad.

Italian Escarole and White Bean Soup

price $15 servings 5 price per serving $3

*T*his is a recipe to whip out on a cool weeknight during the fall. While soups have a reputation for taking forever to prepare, recipes like this one come together incredibly quickly, and the result is a tasty and robust evening dish. Add a strong dose of cayenne and Parmesan for a soup with sharper flavor.

½ cup olive oil

2 garlic cloves, minced

2 14-ounce cans cannellini beans, rinsed

2 bunches escarole, steamed and chopped

5 cups chicken stock

Salt and pepper to taste

Cayenne pepper to taste

½ pound small macaroni, cooked

Parmesan cheese, freshly grated

Heat oil in a large saucepan; sauté garlic 1 minute. Stir in beans, escarole, and stock. Season with salt, pepper, and cayenne pepper. Simmer 5–10 minutes; add macaroni. Serve with Parmesan cheese.

Leftover Chicken Stock

price $10   servings 10   price per serving $1

*T*here are infinite ways to concoct a stock, but this is the one we turn to whenever we've just baked and polished off a chicken. The leftover parts go straight to the pot with vegetables for a fragrant and flavorful stock that we freeze for later.

1 chicken carcass from a baked chicken

8–12 cups water

2 medium onions, quartered

4 carrots, quartered

4 celery stalks, quartered

2 garlic cloves

2 tablespoons herbs (thyme, rosemary, sage, etc.) wrapped and tied in cheesecloth

2 bay leaves

Salt and pepper to taste

Chop chicken carcass into 3"–4" pieces. Put in a large stockpot; add water, onions, carrots, celery, and garlic. Bring to a boil; immediately reduce to a simmer. Skim off fat and foam from surface. Add herbs, bay leaves, and salt and pepper; simmer on low 1 hour. With slotted spoon, remove chicken parts and vegetables. Filter remaining broth through cheesecloth-lined colander into new pot. Use immediately, or freeze for later use.

Miso Soup

price $8   servings 4   price per serving $2

Miso soup is among the simplest, healthiest soups in existence. Though it's known as a Japanese restaurant staple, it's so cheap and easy to make there's no reason it shouldn't be featured regularly at home as well. Alanna's brother drinks a cup of it like tea every night, and we love to serve it for lunch along with a simple green salad.

1 tablespoon fresh ginger, grated
2 cups shitake mushrooms, sliced
5 cups hot water (or dashi stock)
3–5 tablespoons miso paste (to taste)
1 block firm tofu, cut into ¼" cubes
¼ cup green onion, chopped

In a medium bowl, toss ginger and mushrooms with ½ cup water or stock. Steam mushroom mixture in a small pot by bringing to a simmer for 2 minutes. Dissolve miso paste in ½ cup hot water or stock. In a medium pot, combine remaining water or stock, miso mixture, steamed mushrooms, and tofu cubes. Gently simmer about 5 minutes. Sprinkle with green onion before serving.

Roasted Red Pepper Soup

price $18   servings 6   price per serving $3

*F*or a soup with so few ingredients, this one is unbelievably tasty and impressive. Roasting the peppers first creates a sweet, smoky flavor that is complemented beautifully by the subtle tartness and creaminess of the goat cheese. Assembling the croutons and goat cheese bits in the center of the brightly colored soup makes for a stunning presentation.

6 large red bell peppers

3 tablespoons olive oil

2 medium onions, chopped

5 cups chicken stock

⅛ teaspoon dried crushed red pepper flakes

Salt and pepper to taste

3 ounces goat cheese

CROUTONS:

2 tablespoons olive oil

1 teaspoon kosher salt

1 garlic clove, crushed

1 tablespoon rosemary, minced

1½ cups French bread, cut into ½" cubes

Preheat broiler to high. Rub peppers with 1 tablespoon olive oil; arrange on baking sheet. Broil until blackened on all sides, about 20 minutes, turning every 4–5 minutes. Remove and allow to cool in closed paper bag 10 minutes. Peel, seed, and cut peppers into ½" pieces. Heat 2 tablespoons oil in large pot; sauté onion until brown on edges, about 6 minutes. Add peppers; sauté 1 minute. Add stock; bring to a simmer. Cook until vegetables are tender, about 5 minutes. Cool slightly first, then in batches, transfer to a blender and blend until smooth. Mix in red pepper flakes, salt, and pepper. For croutons, preheat oven to 400°F. Combine oil, salt, garlic, and rosemary in a bowl and toss mixture with bread until well coated. Arrange on baking sheet and cook for 15 minutes, until croutons begin to brown. Spoon warm soup into bowls, top with croutons, and top with goat cheese.

Roasted Veggie Gazpacho

price $12   servings 6   price per serving $2

We used to think we loved gazpacho, until we tasted this roasted vegetable version and realized what a love for gazpacho can truly be. With this hot (but still refreshing) version, gazpacho becomes more than a summer soup, since you can roast vegetables year-round. And if you do decide to make this during the summer when the vegetables are in peak season, consider grilling them instead of roasting them.

1 medium tomato, sliced into 1" rounds
2 medium red peppers, halved, seeds removed
2 medium green peppers, halved, seeds removed
1 small eggplant, sliced into ½" rounds
1 small onion, sliced into 1" rounds
2 tablespoons olive oil
Salt and pepper to taste
4 slices bread, Italian or French
3 garlic cloves
8 cups tomato juice
½ teaspoon Tabasco sauce
Juice of 2 lemons
Basil leaves for garnish

Preheat oven to 400°F. Toss tomato, peppers, eggplant, and onion with 2 tablespoons olive oil, salt, and pepper; arrange in a roasting pan and cook 20–25 minutes, until soft and lightly charred. Let vegetables cool and cut into very small pieces. Combine bread and garlic in food processor; pulse until combined. Put bread mixture in large bowl; whisk in tomato juice, Tabasco, and vegetables. Season with salt and pepper and add lemon juice. Serve in soup bowls and garnish with basil leaves.

Rustic Sweet and Sour Cabbage Soup

price $16   servings 4   price per serving $4

This is Alanna's great-grandmother's recipe for a delicious rustic cabbage soup with eastern European flavors that we love during all seasons. It's also embarrassingly easy to prepare—throw the ingredients in a large pot and wait. The only difficult part is resisting the temptation to dig in as soon as the aroma of this homey, familiar soup starts wafting through the house.

1 onion, chopped
1 (28-ounce) can stewed tomatoes
1 (8-ounce) can tomato sauce
1 small head cabbage, thinly sliced
16 ounces sauerkraut
½ cup brown sugar
4 beef bones (optional)
Salt and pepper to taste

Combine all ingredients in a large pot. Fill the tomato cans with water, and add to the pot; cover and bring to a boil. Reduce heat and simmer 2 hours. Adjust seasonings and add more sugar, if needed. Ladle into bowls and serve hot.

Thai Curry Noodle Soup

price $24   servings 6   price per serving $4

*T*his is a dish we'll have for dinner, then want for dessert again a few hours later. The fact that it's creamy and a bit sweet has something to do with it, but we mostly love the way the thick coconut flavor seeps into all of the vegetables.

2 tablespoons vegetable oil

3 chicken breasts, thinly sliced

3 tablespoons yellow curry paste

1" piece ginger, grated

2 carrots, thinly sliced

1 cup shitake mushrooms, sliced

4 cups coconut milk

4 cups chicken stock

Juice of 1 lime

1 teaspoon fish sauce

1 teaspoon soy sauce

1 tablespoon sugar

4 ounces rice noodles

1 head broccoli, cut into small florets

Bean sprouts for garnish

Heat oil in a large pot over medium-high heat. Add chicken; sauté until just browned, about 4 minutes. Stir in curry paste and ginger. Add carrots and mushrooms; continue to cook another 2 minutes. Stir in coconut milk, stock, lime juice, fish sauce, soy sauce, and sugar; bring to a boil. Reduce heat to simmer; cook 15 minutes. Add noodles and broccoli; cook 5 more minutes, until noodles have softened. Ladle into bowls, top with bean sprouts, and serve hot.

Shitake-Soy Barley Soup

price $12 servings 4 price per serving $3

This is not the most beautiful soup in the pot, but it's doable in about an hour, and it still retains the wholesome flavor we love. The shitakes and soy sauce lend an interesting note and complement the other ingredients without overwhelming. Serve alongside dinner rolls or a simple salad.

2 tablespoons olive oil

1 medium onion, sliced

5 carrots, sliced into ¼" pieces

¾ pound button mushrooms, sliced

1 cup barley

1 cup dried shitake mushrooms, soaked in 2 cups hot water
(reserve 1 cup of water)

6 cups chicken broth

Salt and pepper to taste

Soy sauce to taste

Heat olive oil in a large pot. Add onions, carrots, and button mushrooms; sauté until soft. Add barley; sauté 5 minutes. Add shitake mushrooms, chicken broth, and 1 cup water from soaking mushrooms. Bring to boil; lower heat and simmer 45 minutes. Add splash of soy sauce, if you like, and serve.

Nana's Veggie Soup

price $20   servings 10   price per serving $2

This is Alanna's secret family recipe for the best-tasting soup ever. It's been passed down for generations and is served at all holiday dinners. Whenever we feel like healthy, familiar flavors we concoct a batch, savoring the process of slowly simmering vegetables and chicken together to achieve a perfect soup with notes of ginger, carrot, and dill. It freezes beautifully, so cook in advance if you plan to serve a crowd.

1 whole chicken, cut into quarters

5 carrots, peeled and halved

3 parsnips, peeled and halved

Top ⅓ of celery bunch, cut into chunks

1 potato, peeled and cut into chunks

2 onions, quartered

Pinch salt

4 garlic cloves

3" piece ginger, peeled

½ bunch fresh flat-leaf parsley

½ bunch fresh dill

1 12-ounce can stewed tomatoes

½ cup tomato sauce

Salt and pepper to taste

Put all ingredients into a large pot; fill with water until vegetables and chicken are covered. Add salt. Bring to a boil; reduce heat and simmer 2 hours, covered. Remove chicken pieces; set aside for later use (makes great chicken salad). Using a strainer, remove remaining ingredients; separate any leftover chicken from mass of vegetables. Cool slightly, then in a blender, blend vegetables in batches with about 1 cup of broth; return to pot. Season with salt and pepper.

PART I: SMALL DISHES

DiPS

Basil Pesto

price $10   servings 6   price per serving $1.70

*A*lex is convinced that pesto goes on everything. Given his success at sneaking it into dishes, he might be right. This is a classic version with perfectly balanced proportions that can be worked into sandwiches, pastas, and meats.

- 5 cups fresh basil leaves
- 2 garlic cloves, peeled and chopped
- ½ cup olive oil
- ⅓ cup pine nuts, lightly toasted
- ½ cup Parmesan cheese
- 1 teaspoon kosher salt

In a food processor or blender, combine basil, garlic, olive oil, pine nuts, cheese, and salt. Pulse 30 seconds, until smooth.

Punchy Pico de Gallo

price $5   servings 4   price per serving $1.25

*W*e eat this salsa with chips, sandwiches, quesadillas, or, in Alex's case, by the spoonful. It's classic and spicy, but you can add more jalapeño for extra kick.

- 3 medium tomatoes, chopped
- 1 medium red onion, diced
- 1 garlic clove, minced
- ½ jalapeño, diced
- ½ cup fresh cilantro, chopped
- 2 tablespoons olive oil
- Juice of 1 lime
- Salt and pepper to taste

Combine tomatoes, onion, garlic, jalapeño, and cilantro in a bowl. Stir in olive oil and lime juice to coat. Add salt and pepper. Let sit at least 20 minutes before serving.

Guatemalan-Style Guacamole

price $10   servings 4   price per serving $2.25

This is a special guacamole with a secret ingredient: oregano. Though often skeptical before tasting it, everyone who eats this smooth and flavorful dip agrees with us that it's extremely unique and delicious; that is, if they can stop eating long enough to continue the conversation. This is one of our most requested dished, so be warned that once you make it you may not be able to stop making—or eating—it!

> 3 Haas avocados
> Juice of 2 lemons
> ¼ medium onion, chopped
> 2 tablespoons dried oregano
> Salt and pepper to taste

Peel and chop avocados, then mash in a bowl. Add lemon juice and mix. Add onions, oregano, salt, and pepper.

Fruit Salsa with Cinnamon Chips

price $15   servings 10   price per serving $1.50

We share a love for cinnamon pita chips, so it's not surprising that we both became completely hooked on this snack with our first bites. The chips have a perfect crunch and taste amazing with and without the fruit salsa, which itself is independently delicious. We go to this dish for a late-night snack or for parties, but there's no time of day it wouldn't be appropriate.

2 kiwis, peeled and diced
2 Fuji apples, peeled, cored, and diced
8 ounces blackberries
1 pound strawberries, diced
2 tablespoons white sugar
1 tablespoon brown sugar
3 tablespoons strawberry preserves (or other fruit flavor)

CHIPS:
10 (10") flour tortillas
Butter-flavored cooking spray
2 cups cinnamon-sugar

Preheat oven to 350°F. In a large bowl, mix kiwis, apples, blackberries, strawberries, sugars, and preserves. Cover and refrigerate at least 15 minutes. Coat one side of each tortilla with cooking spray. Cut into wedges; arrange on large baking sheet. Coat wedges with desired amount of cinnamon-sugar; spray again with cooking spray. Bake 8–10 minutes; allow to cool approximately 15 minutes. Serve with chilled fruit mixture.

Lemony Hummus

price $4   servings 8   price per serving $.50

*L*ike our guacamole, this is among our most requested recipes, perhaps because we serve it more than anything else. We love it because it somehow turns out extremely light and fluffy, almost as though it has been whipped rather than processed. We add a lot of lemon juice and a little less garlic, but the proportions can easily be adjusted to taste.

2 cans chickpeas (with liquid)
1 clove garlic
½ cup tahini
½ cup lemon juice
1 teaspoon paprika
1 teaspoon salt
¼ teaspoon chili powder
4 tablespoons olive oil

Combine all ingredients in food processor and process until smooth. Spoon into a bowl and serve with pita bread or raw carrots.

Olive Tapenade

price $12   servings 6   price per serving $2

We'd been buying jarred olive tapenade for ages before we discovered that it is cheaper and just as easy to make your own. Now, we do large batches for parties and set it out with raw carrots and chips, just like hummus. You can also use the tapenade as a topping for grilled fish, in sandwiches, or over pasta.

2 cups Kalamata olives, pits removed

3 tablespoons capers

3 tablespoons pine nuts, toasted

½ cup olive oil

2 teaspoons herbes de Provence (or any combination of equal parts rosemary, thyme, oregano, tarragon, and marjoram)

1 teaspoon lemon zest

Pulse olives in food processor until chopped; place in a bowl. Pulse capers until chopped; add to olives. Repeat with pine nuts, processing until ground. Stir in olive oil, herbs de Provence, and lemon zest. Serve with crackers or raw carrots.

Smoky Baba Ghanouj

price **$8**   servings **8**   price per serving **$1**

This baba ghanouj is the perfect dip for a late summer barbeque or gathering. The charred and smoky flavors of the eggplant are truly magical when mixed with tangy lemon juice and creamy tahini. The trick is to grill the eggplant to death—leave it on the grill until the outside is entirely black and soft. Serve it with flatbreads, crackers, or raw vegetables.

2 medium eggplants

½ cup tahini

2 garlic cloves, mashed

Juice of 2 lemons

1 tablespoon pomegranate syrup (you can substitute grenadine if necessary)

Salt to taste

Preheat grill to high. Pierce whole eggplants all over with a fork; place on grill. Grill 40 minutes, or until eggplants are charred black and soft all over, turning every 10 minutes. Remove from grill; place in bath of cold water until cool enough to handle. Remove skin and as many seeds as possible without discarding too much eggplant. Place skinned eggplant in large bowl. Using a fork, shred flesh into small pieces. Stir in tahini, garlic, lemon juice, and pomegranate syrup. Add salt to taste.

Yogurt Spinach Dip

price $6   servings 8   price per serving $.75

This is a dip that tastes much unhealthier than it is. It's as sweet, savory, thick, and satisfying as other spinach dips, but we use plain low-fat yogurt to keep it light.

3 tablespoons olive oil
2 large yellow onions, halved and sliced
9 ounces fresh spinach, steamed and chopped
½ clove garlic, minced
1 cup plain, low-fat yogurt
2 teaspoons honey
Salt and pepper to taste

Heat oil in a large frying pan; add onions. Sauté 15 minutes, stirring occasionally. When onions are very soft and begin to brown, stir more frequently; cook until deep brown and caramelized. Combine spinach, caramelized onions, garlic, and yogurt in medium bowl. Add honey, salt, and pepper. Serve with crackers or sliced bread.

SANDWICHES

Cheddar, Chutney, and Apple Sandwich

price $8   servings 4   price per serving $2

We make this sandwich all the time when we open the refrigerator but don't find cold cuts. While it might seem strange to some that we would find mango chutney but not sliced turkey, it happens more than you'd think, and this sandwich is a simple yet exotic lunch alternative. Any type of apple will do, but we like it best with tart Granny Smiths.

1 baguette
1 jar mango chutney
½ pound sharp Cheddar cheese, sliced
1 apple, cored and sliced

Cut baguette in half lengthwise. Spread with chutney and arrange cheese and apple on one side. Close bread, cut into 4 pieces, and serve. (Alternatively, grill individual sandwiches for a few minutes on each side to melt cheese.)

Curried Egg Salad

price $6   servings 4   price per serving $1.50

When we're making quick lunches like tuna salad or egg salad sandwiches, we have to throw nutrition to the wind and just try to recreate classic deli flavors. Egg salad isn't the healthiest of dishes, but slathered on toasted whole-wheat bread, there's no denying that it's among the tastiest and the least expensive.

12 large eggs, hard-boiled
2 tablespoons mayonnaise
4 teaspoons lemon juice
2 teaspoons chopped red onion
2 teaspoons curry powder
1 teaspoon Worcestershire sauce
Salt and pepper to taste
8 slices whole-wheat bread
4 leaves lettuce

Shell and coarsely chop hard-boiled eggs. In a large bowl, combine eggs, mayonnaise, lemon juice, onion, curry, Worcestershire sauce, salt, and pepper. Adjust salt, pepper, and curry to taste. Assemble sandwiches on toasted whole-wheat bread with lettuce.

Honey-Mustard Grilled Chicken Sandwich

price $12   servings 4   price per serving $3

Alex's obsession with sandwiches extends to (and is, perhaps, intensified by) the genre of grilled sandwiches. Grilling the ingredients is a cost-effective way to transform a regular sandwich into a delectable meal, and the combination of herbs and onions with chicken makes this version perfectly balanced and tasty. This dish is a sophisticated and frugal alternative to hamburgers and hot dogs at your next summer barbeque.

4 chicken breasts
2 tablespoons olive oil
2 garlic cloves, crushed
4 tablespoons honey mustard
2 teaspoons dried rosemary
2 teaspoons dried oregano
2 teaspoons salt
1 teaspoon pepper
1 large Vidalia onion, sliced ½" thick
4 long sandwich rolls
4 ounces crumbled feta cheese

In large bowl, marinate chicken breasts with 1 tablespoon olive oil, crushed garlic, 2 tablespoons honey mustard, rosemary, oregano, salt, and pepper. Place in the refrigerator for about an hour. In a small bowl, toss onion slices in 1 tablespoon olive oil; sprinkle with salt and pepper. On hot grill or large skillet, grill chicken and onions about 4 minutes on each side, until cooked through. Cut chicken into large pieces; fill sandwich rolls. Top with onion, feta, and honey mustard. Serve warm.

New York–Style Turkey Sandwich

price $8   servings 4   price per serving $4

This is Alex's favorite sandwich. Instead of adding coleslaw and dressing, we recommend adding thinly sliced cabbage to avoid a double dose of mayonnaise for a healthier version that stays true to classic deli flavors. Of course, if you have coleslaw on hand, it works just as well.

1½ pounds deli turkey, thinly sliced
½ pound sliced Swiss cheese
8 slices rye bread

RUSSIAN DRESSING:
3 tablespoons mayonnaise
2 tablespoons ketchup
2 teaspoons sweet relish
Dash Worcestershire sauce
1 cup very thinly sliced cabbage

Make dressing in a small bowl by combining mayonnaise, ketchup, relish, and Worcestershire sauce. Mix cabbage with Russian dressing. Assemble sandwiches with turkey, cheese, and cabbage.

Honey, Thyme, Pear, and Goat Cheese Sandwiches

price $10   servings 8   price per serving $1.60

This is one of the first recipes we posted on our blog. Roasting the pears with honey and thyme lends them a distinct savory and sweet taste, and we adore the novelty of using fruit in a sandwich. We usually make these as tea sandwiches for a quick snack, but you can do them full size as well.

2 bunches fresh thyme sprigs
3 Bartlett pears (about 1½ pounds), cored and sliced
¼ cup honey
Salt and pepper to taste
8 slices honey-oat bread
4 ounces goat cheese

Preheat oven to 400°F. Place thyme sprigs on baking sheet; place pear slices on the top. Drizzle pears with honey; sprinkle with salt and pepper. Bake 15 minutes, until pears are tender. Let cool on baking sheet. Lightly toast bread; spread with layer of goat cheese. Arrange pears on half of slices. Form 4 sandwiches and cut each in quarters.

Gruyère Cheese Steak

price $16   servings 4   price per serving $4

We ate a lot of cheese steaks while living in Philadelphia, and we'll defend these to the death as the real thing. Sure, they're lacking fake cheese and grease, but we think that smoky Gruyère layered with mushrooms is just as noteworthy; the spirit is there, and that's what counts.

1 tablespoon olive oil
1 medium onion, thinly sliced
3 cups button mushrooms, thinly sliced
Salt and pepper to taste
1 pound rib-eye steak, thinly sliced
3 ounces Gruyère cheese, grated
4 Italian sandwich rolls

In a large skillet, heat oil; add onion and mushrooms and season with salt and pepper. Cook until onion is caramelized and mushrooms are soft, about 6 minutes; set aside. Add meat to hot skillet; break apart using a spatula. Cook until meat is no longer pink, about 2 minutes. Return onions and mushrooms to pan; mix with meat. Add Gruyère and stir until melted. Add salt and pepper to taste. Fill sandwich rolls with mixture and serve hot.

Open-Face Roasted Veggie Sandwich

price $18   servings   6   price per serving $3

*I*f we saved a nickel every time Alex says, "There's nothing worse than a bad sandwich and nothing better than a great one," we'd have a solid chunk of change. He's a sandwich snob who will turn up his nose unless presented with a perfect balance of fillings, condiments, and bread. His special admiration for this main-course sandwich stems from its attainment of that lofty goal.

2 medium-sized eggplants, sliced into ½-inch rounds
⅔ cup plus ½ cup olive oil
⅓ cup plus ¼ cup balsamic vinegar
1 teaspoon sugar
Salt and pepper to taste
3 medium bell peppers, sliced
3 portobello mushrooms, sliced
2 medium onions, sliced
6 slices thick bread, toasted
Gruyère cheese (optional)

WALNUT BALSAMIC PESTO:
¼ cup walnuts
1 cup basil leaves, chopped
¼ cup olive oil
Salt and pepper to taste

Salt both sides of eggplant slices well; place on pan lined with paper towels. Cover with additional paper towels and leave 20 minutes. Whisk together oil, vinegar, sugar, salt, and pepper. Preheat oven to 400°F. Rinse and dry eggplant; toss with peppers, mushrooms, and onions; toss with olive oil and vinegar. Place on baking sheet; roast 25–30 minutes. Remove mushrooms after 20 minutes; leave other vegetables for remainder of time. To make pesto, combine ingredients in food processor; process until smooth. Spread on bread and top with roasted vegetables. Top with thin strips of Gruyère in a cross-hatch design. Broil about 2 minutes, until cheese melts.

Smoked Salmon Sandwich

price $20   servings 4   price per serving $5

Smoked salmon is often typecast as a topping for bagels only, but it's just as delicious in a sandwich with fresh vegetables. We add both cream cheese and mustard for a surprisingly tasty combination of flavors. You can use thinner bread and cut them into tea sandwiches for guests, but we bet that once you taste one you'll want an entire sandwich to yourself.

8 tablespoons cream cheese
4 teaspoon honey mustard
8 slices rye bread, lightly toasted
8 slices tomato
Handful lettuce leaves
8 thin slices avocado
12 thin slices cucumber
½ pound smoked salmon

Spread cream cheese and mustard on 4 slices of bread. Arrange remaining ingredients and top with second slices of bread.

Spicy Shrimp Salad with Lime and Sprouts

price $16   servings 4   price per serving $4

Alex is a Sriracha fanatic. And while he usually just adds a dash of this Asian hot sauce to any given soup or rice dish, he is particularly fond of this recipe because it incorporates the sauce as a star ingredient. Feel free to use frozen shrimp, which is the most economical (and convenient!) choice.

2 tablespoons mayonnaise
1 teaspoon Sriracha hot sauce or other hot sauce
Juice of 1 lime
1 pound cooked shrimp, shelled, deveined, and cut into ½" pieces
2 tablespoons green onion, chopped
2 leaves romaine lettuce
1 cup bean sprouts
3 long sandwich rolls

In a small bowl, mix together mayonnaise, hot sauce, and lime juice. Toss shrimp with sauce and add green onions. Assemble lettuce, bean sprouts, and shrimp salad on sandwich rolls and serve.

Turkey and Roasted Red Pepper Panini

price $16   servings 4   price per serving $4

Since we eat turkey sandwiches daily, we have many variations to share. This version is great for weekends when you have time to cook the sandwich to perfection. The cheese lends a crucial flavor kick, and we often add extra so it melts down the side of the bread. If you don't have time to cook the sandwich, just throw the ingredients together and eat it on the go.

8 slices pepper jack cheese
8 slices smoked turkey breast
8 slices French bread or ciabatta roll, cut in half
1 roasted red bell pepper or several pieces from a jar
4 teaspoons butter or butter substitute
2 cups mixed greens

Place a slice of cheese and a slice of turkey on each piece of bread. Place a roasted bell pepper on one side of bread and assemble sandwich with pepper in middle. Heat a small pan; spread ½ teaspoon butter on outside of one side of sandwich. When pan is hot, place sandwich in pan. Weigh down with heavy pot; cook about 3 minutes. Remove heavy pot, butter other side of sandwich, flip it; weigh down another 3 minutes, until bread is golden on each side. Remove from pan, slip mixed greens into middle. Repeat and serve.

Cream Cheese and Olive Sandwich

price  $4   servings 4   price per serving $1

This recipe is a throwback to the 1930s. Alex's grandmother used to make these sandwiches when he was young, and he'll defend the strange ingredient combination vehemently for its creamy, salty, and sweet trio of flavors.

8 slices cinnamon raisin bread, toasted
6–8 ounces cream cheese
2 cups pimento olives, sliced

Toast bread and spread cream cheese onto each slice. Arrange olives on each slice and form into sandwiches. Serve for lunch or with tea.

PART II: BIG DISHES

BRUNCH

Apricot–Brandy Baked French Toast

price $12 servings 8 price per serving $1.50

This brunch dish is prepared the night before you serve it, so all you have to do in the morning is pop a baking dish into the oven and wait for heaven to arrive on your plate. The thick, delicious bread is soaked in sugary goodness and baked to a crispy perfection that's both fluffy and delicious. If you don't have apricot brandy on hand, try experimenting with other alcohols, extracts, and toppings like almond extract or hazelnut liqueur.

1 loaf Challah bread, cut into 1" slices
1 cup almonds
3 cups whole milk
3 eggs
3 tablespoons sugar
½ teaspoon salt
3 tablespoons apricot brandy
1 teaspoon vanilla extract
Powdered sugar (optional)

BERRY TOPPING:
2 cups frozen mixed berries
½ cup granulated sugar (or to taste)

Grease 9" × 13" baking dish. Arrange 1 layer of bread slices tightly in pan; sprinkle with ½ cup almonds. Arrange second layer on top; sprinkle with remaining almonds. Whisk together milk, eggs, sugar, salt, brandy, and vanilla; pour over bread. Wrap baking dish tightly with plastic wrap; refrigerate overnight. Bake in 425°F oven 30 minutes, or until puffed and golden. To make berry topping, combine berries and sugar in a saucepan. Bring to a soft boil; simmer 5–10 minutes. Mash to desired consistency. Serve French toast with powdered sugar, berry topping, or both.

Asparagus and Goat Cheese Omelet

price $10   servings 4   price per serving $2.50

*E*very Saturday morning in Philadelphia, we would walk to the Clark Park farmer's market, located just a few blocks from our campus. We'd stop for coffee along the way, then pick up seasonal ingredients for brunch. During the summer months, we'd often grab local goat cheese, asparagus, and farm-fresh eggs for this simple and healthy omelet, which we spruce up with a hint of basil. Serve it alongside slices of multigrain toast.

16 asparagus spears, trimmed and cut into ½" pieces
8 large eggs
½ cup milk
4 tablespoons fresh basil, chopped
1 teaspoon salt
1 teaspoon pepper
2 tablespoon butter
½ cup goat cheese, crumbled

Boil 2 inches of water in medium saucepan. Cook asparagus 3–5 minutes, until slightly softened. Drain in colander and rinse with cold water; set aside. In a mixing bowl, beat together eggs, milk, basil, salt, and pepper. Melt butter in medium nonstick skillet over medium heat. Pour in ¼ egg mixture; cook until almost set, 2–3 minutes. Add handful asparagus spears and ¼ of the goat cheese to slightly runny eggs; cook 1 more minute. Fold omelet in half and cook until set. Remove from pan, repeat for other 3 omelets, and serve warm.

Baked Eggs with Ham and Leeks

price $8   servings 4   price per serving $2

We recreated this dish after tasting a similar version at an idyllic bed and breakfast in Nova Scotia. It's a great brunch item for crowds since you bake the eggs in individual portions, and the presentation is simple and memorable.

2 tablespoons butter
2 large leeks, whites only, sliced
4 slices breakfast ham, deli ham, or prosciutto, chopped
4 large eggs
Salt and pepper to taste

Preheat oven to 375°F. In frying pan, melt 1 tablespoon butter on medium heat; add leeks and cook 8–10 minutes, until soft. Add ham; cook additional 2–3 minutes and set aside. Grease 4 ramekins with remaining 1 tablespoon butter. Distribute leek and ham mixture between ramekins. Crack 1 egg into each ramekin; season lightly with salt and pepper. Bake 10–15 minutes, until egg is set and yolk is slightly runny. Serve immediately.

Chocolate-Berry Oatmeal Brulée

price **$6**   servings **4**   price per serving **$1.50**

We're not huge fans of plain oatmeal, but add a few goodies and it's a different dish altogether. The caramelized sugar makes the dish feel like a real treat, and we love how it crunches into the soft fresh fruit and melting chocolate. Though this is classically a brunch item, we can't help but sneak it in for an afternoon snack or dessert as well.

1 tablespoon butter, melted
1 cups mixed berries (strawberries, raspberries, blueberries)
½ cup chocolate chips
4 cups plain oatmeal, cooked according to package
½ teaspoon cinnamon
¼ cup dark brown sugar

Preheat broiler. Mix butter, berries, and chocolate chips into oatmeal. Combine cinnamon and brown sugar in a small bowl. Butter 4 ramekins and scoop oatmeal mixture into them. Sprinkle brown sugar and cinnamon mixture on top of each; broil 3–4 minutes, until brown sugar starts to bubble. Serve hot.

Cinnamon-Cranberry-Orange Oat Scones

price $15   servings 18   price per serving $.85

Although we bake scones regularly, we are always shocked that we are able to achieve the flaky, buttery texture that we love so much in bakery-bought versions. But again and again we're reminded that homemade scones are easy to make and, considering the low price, absolutely worth it. The cranberry-orange combination in these scones gives them an especially fresh and light taste despite the high butter content, which we think you'll agree is worth the calories.

4⅔ cups all-purpose flour

1 cup granulated sugar, plus some to sprinkle

1 teaspoon cinnamon

1½ teaspoons baking powder

1½ teaspoons kosher salt

Zest of 2 oranges, finely chopped

3 cups old-fashioned oats

2 cups (4 sticks) cold, unsalted butter, cut into small cubes

1½ cups dried cranberries

1½ cups buttermilk

2 tablespoons heavy cream or whipping cream

In a large bowl, combine flour, sugar, cinnamon, baking powder, salt, orange zest, and oats; add butter and toss. On low speed, beat mixture until it becomes a coarse meal; stir in cranberries. Add buttermilk; mix with spoon until it comes together as a dough. Scoop onto floured surface; press into a ball, then divide in thirds. Press each third into ¾" disk, wrap each one with plastic wrap, and refrigerate at least 2 hours, or overnight. Preheat oven to 375°F. Unwrap disks; cut each into 6 equal wedges; divide among 2 greased or nonstick baking sheets, 2" apart. Brush cream over; sprinkle with granulated sugar. Bake sheets 1 at a time on center rack 25–30 minutes, until lightly golden. Serve slightly warm.

Cinnamon–Sweet Potato Waffles

price ($12)   servings (6)   price per serving ($2)

*T*hough we originally cooked this delicious sweet and savory treat for an evening meal, it works best as a brunch item in the fall, when sweet potatoes are in season. Top it with pecans, walnuts, or even mashed sweet potatoes with maple syrup.

2 cups whole-wheat flour

¼ cup brown sugar

4 teaspoons baking soda

1 teaspoon cinnamon

½ teaspoon apple pie spice

1½ cups skim milk

2 eggs

1½ cups sweet potato, cooked and mashed

1 teaspoon orange zest

¼ cup butter or butter substitute, melted

½ cup walnuts, toasted

Sliced bananas and maple syrup for topping

Combine flour, sugar, baking soda, cinnamon, and apple pie spice in a large bowl. In a small bowl, whisk together milk, eggs, sweet potato, orange zest, and butter. Pour liquid batter over dry mixture; mix in walnuts. Pour batter into lightly greased waffle maker; cook until slightly brown, 5–7 minutes. Top with sliced bananas and maple syrup.

Cooked Cherry Parfait

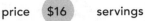

price $16   servings 4   price per serving $4

This recipe will satisfy your cravings any time of day. We adore it for afternoon snack, but the combination of crunchy granola with juicy fruit and smooth yogurt will delight your taste buds at breakfast, brunch, or even dessert. Make it during the summer, when cherries are fresh, sweet, and plump.

4 handfuls fresh cherries, halved and pitted
2 tablespoons sugar
24 ounces vanilla yogurt
4 ounces granola

Add cherries and 3 tablespoons water to small pan; cook over medium heat. Cook 2 minutes, until cherries release their natural juices. Stir in sugar; cook additional 1 minute, until juice become syrupy. Remove from heat. Divide yogurt between 4 glasses; spoon granola over yogurt. Divide remaining yogurt; spoon into glasses and top with cherries and their syrup.

Fresh Veggie Frittata

price $10   servings 4   price per serving $2.50

The first time we made a frittata, we didn't realize it would rise; and thanks to some minor overflow, we accidentally made scrambled eggs on the bottom of the oven in addition to our gorgeous vegetable frittata. Since that mishap, we've made this frittata many times with perfect execution, resulting in a fluffy and flavorful meal that's particularly excellent for summer nights and lazy brunches.

2 tablespoons olive oil
1 medium onion, halved and sliced
1 medium potato, peeled and sliced
Salt and pepper to taste
1 red bell pepper, sliced
2 cups fresh spinach, packed
4 whole eggs
4 egg whites
1 teaspoon salt
1 teaspoon black pepper
1 teaspoon dried oregano
½ cup Parmesan cheese, grated

Preheat oven to 350°F. Heat 1 tablespoon olive oil in pan; sauté onion, potato, salt, and pepper 10 minutes. Add red pepper; cook 5 minutes. Steam spinach and set aside. In a bowl, whisk eggs, egg whites, salt, pepper, and oregano together. In 8" × 8" baking dish, layer ½ of spinach, ½ of vegetable mixture, and ½ cheese. Add ½ of egg mixture. Layer remaining spinach, vegetables, and cheese; pour remaining egg on top. Bake 20 minutes, until eggs are cooked through. Cool and serve.

Leftover Rice Pudding

price $5 servings 5 price per serving $1

The next time you find yourself staring down a carton of leftover rice in the fridge, transform it into this delectable frugal goodie—rice coated in warm vanilla, sugar, and spices, stirred gently into a thick and aromatic pudding. We recommend using soy milk, especially the vanilla-flavored variety, but you can use skim or whole milk, too.

2 cups leftover cooked white rice
3 cups soy milk (or skim or whole)
½ cup sugar
Small pinch salt
1 teaspoon vanilla extract
2 cinnamon sticks
½ teaspoon cinnamon
Pinch nutmeg (optional)

Combine cooked rice, milk, sugar, and salt in medium saucepan. Bring to a boil; lower to simmer. Stir in vanilla and add cinnamon sticks. Cook until almost all of milk is absorbed, 30–45 minutes. Stir in cinnamon and nutmeg and serve.

Mango and Honey Greek Yogurt Parfait

price $8   servings 4   price per serving $2

This parfait is a great use for tangy, creamy Greek yogurt, and using the fat-free variety makes this dessert as healthy as it is delicious. We've experimented with mango and banana, but any fruit you have on hand will work.

1 large container (20-ounce) fat-free Greek yogurt
¼ cup honey
2 mangoes, cubed

Layer two spoonfuls of yogurt in a glass. Drizzle with honey, add cubed mango pieces, and repeat.

Sweet Cinnamon Cottage Cheese

price $3   servings 4   price per serving $.75

We've tried adding cinnamon-sugar to many foods, and often with less-than-noteworthy results. But somehow, adding this timeless combination to cottage cheese induces a miraculous transformation in an otherwise drab food. We get a lot of raised eyebrows for this one, but we swear it makes the cottage cheese taste like cheesecake.

2 cups cottage cheese   1½ tablespoon sugar
1 teaspoon cinnamon   2 tablespoons raisins

In a small bowl, combine cottage cheese, cinnamon, sugar, and raisins. Serve on toast for a hearty breakfast or tasty snack.

Midnight Cornmeal Pancakes

price $12   servings 4   price per serving $3

We love to make these mouth-watering pancakes for dinner, breakfast, lazy weekend brunches, or even midnight snacks. Sometimes we even travel with Jiffy mix so we can make them wherever we go. They're perfect for crowds and delicious as cold finger food the next day. Just add a drop of maple syrup or a sprinkle of powdered sugar for the yummiest pancake in the world.

1 box corn muffin mix (Jiffy brand works well)

2 eggs

¾ cup milk

2 tablespoons butter, melted (plus more for greasing pan)

2 bananas, cut up

1 cup chopped pecans

1 tablespoon butter

Maple syrup

Mix together cornmeal mix, eggs, milk, and melted butter in large bowl. Add bananas and pecans; mash banana chunks into mixture. Heat 1 tablespoon butter in frying pan on medium-high heat. Spoon mixture onto pan according to desired size of pancakes. When they start bubbling on top, flip them; cook 2–3 minutes on each side. Serve immediately with maple syrup.

Purple Potato Spanish Tortilla

price **$10**   servings **4**   price per serving **$2.50**

Whenever we see vegetables in strange colors, we can't help but buy them. We've come home with purple peppers, purple and yellow cauliflower, and white eggplant, to name a few. The purple potatoes in this Spanish tortilla make it look a bit unusual, but we've kept the traditional flavor and essence intact. But if you can't find purple potatoes, any potato will do!

5 tablespoons olive oil, divided

3 purple potatoes, thinly sliced

1 red onion, thinly sliced

Salt and pepper to taste

9 eggs

Heat 3 tablespoons olive oil in a large pan. Add potatoes and onions with salt and pepper; cook 15 minutes, or until ingredients are soft. Beat eggs in large bowl 2 minutes. Pour potatoes and onions into bowl; fold into eggs. Add remaining 2 tablespoons olive oil to pan; pour mixture back into pan. Cook on stove over medium heat 10 minutes, or until eggs have almost set. Preheat broiler; broil 1 minute, until eggs are firm. Remove tortilla from pan; cool to room temperature before serving.

Slow-Cooked Rosemary Scrambled Eggs

price **$10**   servings **4**   price per serving **$2.50**

If you have a minute to spare in the morning, try this recipe for scrambled eggs that are far superior to regular scrambled eggs. After making them once, you'll say goodbye to memories of dry, gummy eggs and welcome a new version—creamy, soft, and delicious with a hint of fresh herbs.

8 eggs
4 tablespoon milk
2 teaspoon olive oil, divided
Salt and pepper to taste
4 stems fresh rosemary
4 ounces goat cheese

Whisk eggs, milk, 1 teaspoon olive oil, salt, and pepper together in a bowl. Heat remaining olive oil in a pan over low heat; add egg mixture and rosemary stems. Cook over low heat, stirring constantly, 5 minutes, or until eggs are cooked. Stir in goat cheese during last 30 seconds. Remove rosemary stems. Serve hot.

POULTRY

Roasted Chicken with Tomatoes and Potatoes

price $20   servings 4   price per serving $5

*T*his is a simple and healthy weeknight recipe, made a little bit special by a tasty gravy that goes deliciously over the chicken and vegetables without overwhelming them. It's a main-course dish served along with a simple salad.

2 red onions, quartered
½ pound new potatoes, quartered
2 Roma tomatoes, quartered
2 yellow tomatoes, quartered
1 cup Kalamata olives, pitted
¼ cup fresh rosemary, coarsely chopped
¼ cup fresh thyme leaves
4 tablespoons olive oil, divided
1 whole chicken, cut into parts
Salt and pepper to taste
Juice of 1 lemon
1½ cups chicken broth
1 tablespoon flour
1 tablespoon whole-grain mustard

Preheat oven to 375°F. In large bowl, combine onions, potatoes, tomatoes, olives, rosemary, and thyme; toss with 2 tablespoons oil. Rub remaining 2 tablespoons oil over chicken; sprinkle with salt and pepper. Arrange chicken in large baking dish; surround with potatoes, tomatoes, onions, and olives. Squeeze lemon juice on top; bake 20 minutes. Pour chicken broth over top; cook 45 minutes to 1 hour, until cooked through. Remove from oven; carefully pour pan juices into saucepan and skim fat. Heat on low heat; whisk in flour, mustard, salt, and pepper. Simmer 5 minutes; remove from heat. Serve chicken and vegetables topped with pan gravy.

Top-Secret Turkey Chili

price $18   servings 6   price per serving $3

Alex learned this method of chili preparation from a close friend and mastermind chili chef. Because it's a method, let the recipe act as a guidebook rather than an instruction manual. We traditionally make a batch every fall, and the flavors are hot enough to warm the soul as well as the body. It's perfect comfort food for curling up with a good book or for serving with beer and guacamole to friends.

6 tablespoons olive oil
1 onion, chopped
2 garlic cloves, minced
1½ pounds ground turkey
1 tablespoon chili powder
½ tablespoon oregano
Salt and pepper to taste
2 bell peppers, chopped
½ jalapeño pepper, seeds removed, chopped
1 (29-ounce) can diced tomatoes
1 (29-ounce) can black beans
1 (29-ounce) can red kidney beans
1 (29-ounce) can pinto beans
Cheddar cheese, shredded, for garnish
Cilantro, chopped, for garnish

Heat 3 tablespoons olive oil in a large pot; sauté onions and garlic 5 minutes. Add ground turkey; cook additional 5–7 minutes. Season with chili powder, oregano, salt, and pepper. Add bell and jalapeño peppers; cook until softened. Add tomatoes and beans; simmer 30 minutes. Adjust seasonings to taste. Garnish with cheese and cilantro and serve.

Barbeque Chicken Pizza

price $20   servings 4   price per serving $5

This alternative to classic pizza substitutes barbeque sauce for tomato sauce and Gouda for mozzarella, resulting in a sweet and smoky pizza pie that will make you question any loyalties you may have harbored toward more traditional varieties. Use a spicy barbeque sauce to add heat or sprinkle a few red pepper flakes over the top. During the summer, throw the chicken on the grill instead of opting for the pan-cooked version.

2 tablespoons olive oil

3 boneless chicken breasts

Salt and pepper to taste

⅔ cup barbecue sauce

1 recipe Homemade Pizza Crust (see page 136)

7 ounces smoked Gouda cheese, coarsely shredded

1 onion, thinly sliced

1 scallion, chopped

Preheat oven to 500°F. Heat oil in a skillet. Season chicken with salt and pepper; sauté until just cooked through, about 5 minutes per side. Transfer to plate to rest 5 minutes before slicing into strips. In a bowl, toss with ½ cup barbecue sauce. Roll out pizza dough; fit onto large baking sheet. Spread ½ of cheese over dough. Arrange chicken on dough; sprinkle onions on top. Drizzle pizza with remaining barbecue sauce; sprinkle with remaining cheese and scallions. Bake until cheese melts and crust is crisp, about 14 minutes. Remove from oven and serve hot.

Blue Cheese Inside-Out Turkey Burgers

price $12   servings 4   price per serving $3

*T*he concept here is a cheeseburger with cheese already incorporated into the burger. There's no need to melt an extra slice on top because these already have the melted, gooey smoothness of a cheeseburger built in. And whereas turkey burgers can sometimes turn out dry, the blue cheese keeps these incredibly moist and tasty. The idea can apply to beef burgers as well.

1¼ pounds lean ground turkey
1 onion, finely diced
1 garlic clove, diced
6 ounces blue cheese, crumbled (¾ cup)
¼ cup unseasoned bread crumbs
1 tablespoon Worcestershire sauce
¼ cup fresh flat-leaf parsley, chopped
1 teaspoon salt
½ teaspoon pepper
4 hamburger buns
Lettuce, sliced tomato, and sliced onion (optional)

In a large bowl, combine turkey, onion, garlic, blue cheese, and bread crumbs. Mix in Worcestershire sauce, parsley, salt, and pepper. Preheat the grill or a large skillet. Form 4 patties; grill 4 minutes on each side, until cooked through. Serve on a toasted bun with fixings, if desired.

"C" Spice-Rub Chicken

price $10   servings 4   price per serving $2.50

You don't need a recipe to whip up this delicious rub for grilled chicken. Just head to your spice rack and combine a teaspoon of every spice that begins with the letter "C." You'll end up with a complex and creative rub that's great for coating chicken (or roast pork, pork chops, or any other meat). This recipe could cost more or less than the estimated amount based on the number of spices you have in your pantry.

1 whole chicken, cut into quarters and pat dry
½ teaspoon cinnamon
1 teaspoon brown sugar
1 teaspoon kosher salt
1 teaspoon coarsely ground black pepper
1 teaspoon cayenne pepper
1 teaspoon cumin
1 teaspoon coriander
1 teaspoon curry
1 teaspoon celery seed
1 teaspoon ground chipotle pepper
1 teaspoon cardamom
1 teaspoon chili powder

Preheat grill. Combine all dry ingredients in a bowl. Rub mixture into chicken pieces. Grill chicken 5 minutes on each side or longer for thicker chicken breasts, until cooked through.

Chicken with Figs and Rosemary Wine Sauce

price $25   servings 4   price per serving  $6.25

We wish we could make this dish every night, but, unfortunately, truly beautiful fresh and plump figs are only available in late summer. While they are available at specialty food markets, we've also found them at fruit carts on the streets of New York for only a few dollars per pound. This recipe incorporates the sweet fig juice into a syrupy wine sauce with paprika and fresh rosemary. The chicken turns out incredibly moist and requires no marinating, which is why we love it for dinner parties.

4 chicken breasts
1 teaspoon paprika, divided
Salt and pepper to taste
2 tablespoons olive oil
1½ cups red wine
20 fresh figs, halved
2 tablespoons fresh rosemary, coarsely chopped

Sprinkle chicken with ½ teaspoon paprika, salt, and pepper. Heat oil in a large pan; add chicken and brown on both sides, about 2 minutes per side. Add wine and figs; sprinkle rosemary and remaining paprika on top. Turn heat to medium; cover and cook until chicken is cooked through, 12–15 minutes. Move chicken to plate and cover. Reduce wine and fig sauce uncovered additional 5 minutes, until thickened. Divide chicken among plates and pour sauce on top.

Classic Colombian Arroz con Pollo

price　$30　servings　6　price per serving　$5

*E*very member of Alex's family ranks this dish among their all-time favorites. His family has perfected the recipe for this classic dish, bursting with bright colors and South American flavors. There's no way to taste this version and resist raving about it. Plus, it only requires one pan, which means less time for cleaning and more time for second and third helpings.

1 tablespoon olive oil
2 pounds chicken breasts and thighs
1 medium green pepper, chopped
1 medium red pepper, chopped
1 medium onion, chopped
2 garlic cloves, minced
Pinch saffron
1 teaspoon paprika
½ teaspoon cumin
1½ cups rice
3 cups chicken broth
½ cup pimento olives, chopped
2 tablespoons capers
½ cup roasted red peppers, chopped
1 cup frozen green peas
Salt and pepper to taste

In a deep pan, heat olive oil on medium-high heat; brown chicken 4 minutes on each side. Remove and set aside. Add peppers, onions, and garlic to pan; cook until soft. Mix in saffron, paprika, cumin, and rice; stir until rice is coated, about 1 minute. Add chicken broth; return chicken to pan. Cover tightly; simmer on medium heat 15–20 minutes, until most of broth is absorbed. Add olives, capers, roasted red peppers, peas, salt, and pepper; stir and let cook 5 minutes uncovered. Serve hot.

Lemon and Herb–Roasted Chicken

price **$16**   servings **4**   price per serving **$4**

*S*imple and classic, we make this chicken for dinner at least once a week. Not only is it healthy, easy, and delicious, this roasting chicken fills our kitchen with the homiest and most irresistible aroma of vegetables and lemony meat. Use the freshest herbs available, and remember to save leftovers for chicken stock.

1 (4–5 pound) whole chicken
3 medium onions, cut in quarters
4 carrots, chopped into ½" pieces
2 pounds small red potatoes, quartered
2 tablespoons olive oil
3 tablespoons fresh rosemary, chopped
3 tablespoons fresh thyme, chopped
1 tablespoon kosher salt
1 tablespoon pepper
5 garlic cloves, minced
1 lemon

Preheat oven to 375°F. Wash chicken and pat dry; place in a roasting pan. In a bowl, combine vegetables and olive oil. Mix ½ of rosemary and thyme, salt, and pepper into vegetables. Rub remaining rosemary and thyme and garlic over chicken and under skin. Squeeze lemon juice over chicken, then place in chicken cavity. Sprinkle salt and pepper over chicken. Arrange vegetables around chicken in roasting pan; cook 20 minutes per pound, or until juices run clear when thigh is pierced and internal temperature of the breast meat is 165°F. Let chicken rest 5 minutes before carving.

Jamaican-Style Roasted Chicken

price $15   servings 5   price per serving $3

We know that we'll never grow tired of cooking because there will always be new ways to roast a chicken. This preparation yields a chicken that is hot, sweet, and busting with flavor. It goes beautifully over couscous or rice.

⅛ cup soy sauce
¼ cup teriyaki sauce
2 tablespoons curry powder
½ teaspoon cayenne pepper
⅛ teaspoon cinnamon
¼ cup brown sugar
4 carrots, cut into 1" pieces
3 onions, quartered
1 (5–6 pound) roasting chicken

Mix together soy sauce, teriyaki sauce, curry, cayenne, cinnamon, and brown sugar. Arrange carrots and onions around chicken in roasting pan. Rub marinade over chicken; bake in 350°F oven 1½ hours, or until juices run clear.

Paprika Chicken Quesadillas

price $12   servings 4   price per serving $3

Quesadillas are often staples for quick lunches and dinners, and it doesn't take much to kick this relatively simple dish into a truly exciting and flavorful meal. Seasoning the chicken for only 10 minutes in advance makes a world of difference and eliminates the need for adding toppings like sour cream later on.

4 tablespoons olive oil

2 chicken breasts

1 teaspoon paprika

1½ teaspoons chili powder, divided

½ teaspoon salt

½ teaspoon pepper

1 medium red bell pepper, sliced

1 medium onion, sliced

4 large flour tortillas

8 ounces shredded cheese (Cheddar and pepper jack work well)

Preheat grill or preheat large skillet with 1 tablespoon olive oil. Place chicken in plastic bag; add paprika, 1 teaspoon chili powder, salt, and pepper. Marinate up to 10 minutes. Grill on medium heat 6–8 minutes per side, or sauté 6 minutes per side. Heat 2 tablespoons olive oil in pan; add pepper and onion. Cook over medium heat 10–15 minutes, or until vegetables are very soft. Add ½ teaspoon chili powder and salt and pepper to taste; set aside. Add 1 tablespoon oil to pan. Lay a tortilla flat in pan; add layer of cheese, peppers, onions, and chicken on one side of tortilla. Fold other side of tortilla on top. Cook 2–3 minutes on each side, or until cheese melts. Serve with guacamole, salsa, or sour cream.

Pizza with Spicy Turkey Sausage

price $18   servings 4   price per serving $4.50

This recipe is our healthier alternative to takeout sausage pizza. Spicy turkey sausage is inexpensive and available almost anywhere. We also add it to pasta with melted cheese and tomato sauce, for "pizza noodles" with spicy turkey sausage.

> 2 tablespoons olive oil
>
> 1 pound spicy turkey sausage, sliced
>
> 1 recipe Homemade Pizza Crust (see page 136)
>
> ⅔ cup marinara sauce
>
> 2 cups mozzarella cheese, coarsely shredded
>
> 1 medium red bell pepper, thinly sliced
>
> 1 medium onion, thinly sliced

Preheat oven to 500°F. Heat oil in skillet; sauté sausage until just cooked through, about 5 minutes. Remove from heat and set aside. Roll out dough; place on large baking sheet. Spread sauce over dough; sprinkle with ½ of cheese. Arrange sausage, peppers, and onions over dough; sprinkle with remaining cheese. Bake until cheese melts and crust is crisp, about 14 minutes. Let cool slightly and serve.

Prosciutto and Parmesan Roll

price ($20)   servings (4)   price per servi[ng]

*T*his pan-cooked chicken is full of flavor and punch. Fe[ed] white wine you have on hand. We buy a bunch of cheap [bottles when] they go on sale and keep them around the kitchen for cook[in]g these kinds of dishes.

4 boneless chicken breasts
4 slices prosciutto
4 tablespoons Parmesan cheese, grated
8 basil leaves
¼ cup flour
Salt and pepper to taste
3 tablespoons olive oil
1½ cups white wine

On a cutting board, pound chicken breasts flat with a kitchen hammer or rolling pin. Place 1 slice prosciutto, 1 tablespoon Parmesan, and 2 basil leaves on each breast. Roll up chicken breasts and secure with wooden toothpicks. Roll each breast through flour to lightly coat; season with salt and pepper. In large pan heat olive oil and sauté chicken over medium heat until golden brown on all sides. Add 1 cup wine to pan; cover and reduce heat. Simmer 15–20 minutes, turning several times, until chicken is tender and cooked through. Remove from pan; increase heat and add remaining ½ cup wine. Deglaze skillet and reduce liquid to form sauce. Season with salt and pepper, spoon over chicken, and serve.

Roasted Chicken with Apple, Onion, and Leek Stuffing

price $15 servings 4 price per serving $3.75

*S*ometimes when we feel like mixing up our traditional weeknight dinner of roasted chicken, we'll throw in a stuffing with seasonal ingredients. This is Alex's favorite version of stuffing, and he substitutes onions for leeks when leeks are out of season.

2 tablespoons olive oil
1 medium onion, chopped
2 leeks, chopped
2 apples, chopped
½ teaspoon dried sage
1 teaspoon dried parsley
½ teaspoon dried thyme
Salt and pepper to taste
½ cup walnuts, chopped
1 cup day-old bread, cubed
¾ cup chicken stock
1 (4–5 pound) whole roasting chicken

Preheat oven to 350°F. For stuffing, heat olive oil in large skillet; add onions and leeks. Cook until soft; add apples, sage, parsley, thyme, salt, and pepper. Cook 2 minutes; stir in walnuts and bread. Slowly add stock; sauté until stock is absorbed. Wash and pat chicken dry. Place in roasting pan; stuff with apple, onion, and leek stuffing. Season with salt and pepper; bake 20 minutes per pound, or until chicken juices run clear and the internal temperature of the breast meat is 165°F.

Roasted Chicken Wrapped with Bacon

price $15   servings 5   price per serving $3

This recipe is from the brilliant mind of Alex's uncle Rob, who has a knack for making the most moist chicken—no matter how he cooks it. This recipe is no exception, as the fat from the bacon keeps the chicken soft and tender. And the drippings make a stellar bacon-flavored gravy.

3 medium onions, quartered
1 (4–5 pound) whole roasting chicken
¼ pound strip bacon
Salt and pepper to taste

Preheat oven to 400°F. Arrange onions around chicken in a roasting pan; place some onion into chicken cavity. Cover chicken with several strips of bacon; sprinkle with salt and pepper. Bake 30 minutes at 400°F, then lower to 350°F until cooked through and breast meat is 165°F, about 1 hour.

Savory Turkey Meatball

price 〔$8〕 servings 〔4〕 price per serving 〔$2〕

Around 3 p.m. each weekday, we begin chatting from work or school about what to cook for dinner. We developed this recipe one evening after Alanna had announced definitively during the day that she wanted spaghetti and meatballs for dinner. We've gone back and reworked the recipe to perfection—the meatballs have a slightly smoky flavor from the cumin, and they're especially soft if you use homemade bread crumbs.

1 teaspoon kosher salt
½ teaspoon pepper
½ teaspoon cumin
½ teaspoon thyme
½ cup seasoned bread crumbs
2 tablespoons Parmesan cheese, grated
1½ pounds lean ground turkey
½ onion, diced
2 eggs
1 teaspoon Worcestershire sauce
Juice of 1 lemon

Preheat oven to 350°F. Lightly grease baking sheet. In a large bowl, mix together salt, pepper, cumin, thyme, bread crumbs, and Parmesan. Add turkey, onion, eggs, Worcestershire sauce, and lemon juice. Mix ingredients together with a fork until well combined. Roll into 2" balls; place on baking sheet. Bake 25–30 minutes. Serve warm with spaghetti and marinara sauce.

Sun-Dried Tomato and Pesto Chicken Wheels

price $20   servings 4   price per serving $5

We're always excited to discover new ways to mix up the pesto and sun-dried tomato combination because we never tire of it. This recipe calls for rolling chicken breasts around this power duo. It's a timeless technique that anyone can do, and the pesto keeps the chicken breasts nice and moist.

4 chicken breasts, pounded flat between 2 sheets of wax paper
½ cup pesto
½ cup sun-dried tomatoes, chopped
1 tablespoon olive oil
Salt and pepper to taste

Preheat oven to 350°F degrees. Prepare chicken by spreading pesto evenly over each breast. Place sun-dried tomatoes over pesto; loosely roll each breast. Place in baking dish seam-side down. Brush with olive oil and season with salt and pepper. Bake 1 hour.

PART II: BIG DISHES
MEAT

Braised Beef Short Ribs

price $24   servings 6   price per serving $4

This dish will fill your home with the savory and homey aroma of short ribs that are so succulent you'll hardly be able to wait for them to finish cooking before digging in.

1 bottle red wine
2 tablespoons olive oil
6 beef short ribs (about 2 pounds)
Salt and pepper to taste
2 medium onions, chopped
2 carrots, chopped
2 stalks celery, chopped
3 garlic cloves, chopped
1 tablespoon whole black peppercorns
1 bay leaf
4 fresh thyme sprigs
4 cups chicken, veal, or beef stock

Preheat oven to 350°F. Add wine to large saucepan; simmer until reduced by half. Heat oil in large sauté or roasting pan. Season ribs with salt and pepper. Add to pan; brown well on both sides. Remove; set aside. Drain all but 1 tablespoon oil from pan. Add vegetables, garlic, peppercorns, bay leaf, and thyme; cook until lightly browned. Add reduced wine; deglaze pan and return ribs to pan. Cover with chicken stock and bring to a simmer. Cover; place in oven and cook 2½ hours, until tender. Remove pan from oven; allow to cool several hours or overnight. Remove excess fat; return pan to stove over medium heat. Simmer uncovered until liquid is reduced by ¾, about 1 hour. Spoon gravy over top of ribs and serve.

Braised Pork Chops with Apples and Leeks

price $10   servings 4   price per serving $2.50

*D*uring the fall, we'll throw apples and leeks on any ingredient that falls into our hands (like the chicken stuffing on page 96). Pork chops handle the flavor combination exquisitely, and the apple cider in this dish enhances the flavor of both the apples and the meat.

4 pork chops

Salt and pepper to taste

2 tablespoons olive oil

2 Granny Smith apples, peeled, cored, and thinly sliced

3 leeks, whites only, sliced

1 teaspoon dried thyme

1 cup apple cider

Fresh flat-leaf parsley for garnish

Season each pork chop generously with salt and pepper. Heat olive oil in large skillet on medium-high heat. Add pork chops; sear until browned, about 3 minutes each side. Remove, cover, and set aside. Add apples, leeks, and thyme to pan; cook until soft. Add cider; simmer 3 minutes, until slightly thickened. Return pork chops to pan; simmer on low heat until cooked through. Season sauce with salt and pepper and garnish with parsley.

Chunky Beef and Veggie Stew

price $30   servings 8   price per serving $3.75

This is a basic, frugal recipe for a hearty beef stew. The wild mushrooms and rosemary lend a rustic touch, and it freezes beautifully to last you through the winter.

3 pounds beef chuck, cubed

3 tablespoons flour

1 tablespoon olive oil

1 medium onion, chopped

3 cups red wine

3 cups beef stock

2 tablespoons tomato paste

1 tablespoon rosemary leaves, chopped

1 tablespoon herbes de Provence (or any combination of equal parts rosemary, thyme, oregano, tarragon, and marjoram)

8 ounces wild mushrooms

4 carrots, sliced

2 cups pearl onions, peeled

2 cups frozen peas

Salt and pepper to taste

Preheat oven to 350°F. Dredge beef in flour. In wide, heavy pot or Dutch oven, sauté beef in olive oil. Add onions; cook over high heat until soft. Add wine, stock, tomato paste, and herbs. Bake 1½ hours. Meanwhile, sauté mushrooms, carrots, and onions until slightly soft, 5–7 minutes, and set aside. Add to pot carrots, pearl onions, mushrooms, peas, and salt and pepper to taste; return to oven 30 minutes. Remove from oven and serve hot.

Coffee-Flavored Grilled Steak

price $16   servings 4   price per serving $4

While this steak doesn't taste like coffee, it *does* take on a uniquely delicious flavor that we've found unachievable with any other ingredient.

1½ pounds steak (top sirloin, chuck eye, flank, or hanger steak)	¼ cup coarsely ground black pepper
¼ cup kosher salt	¼ cup finely ground coffee

Sprinkle steak liberally with salt; cover with pepper and press into steak by hand. Sprinkle finely ground coffee over steak; grill or broil until done, 4–5 minutes on each side depending on thickness and desired temperature. Serve with a pasta salad or simple green salad.

Sweet and Sour Meatloaf

price $16   servings 4   price per serving $4

This is a meatloaf that's juicy and flavorful, with a thick, sweet sauce you'll want to lick off the plate. Leftovers are unlikely, but the meatloaf also makes delicious sandwiches if you manage to save any.

2 pounds lean ground beef	¼ cup brown sugar
1 cup onion, chopped	Juice of 1 lemon
1 egg	1 small can San Arturo tomato mushroom sauce (or substitute other tomato sauce)
½ cup seasoned bread crumbs	

Preheat oven to 350°F. In a large bowl, mix together meat, onion, egg, and bread crumbs. Form into a loaf on baking sheet. Mix together brown sugar, lemon juice, and tomato mushroom sauce; pour over loaf. Bake 1 hour.

Slow-Cooked Corned Beef and Veggies

price  $24   servings 6   price per serving $4

*I*n this recipe, we combine corned beef with a variety of spices and rustic vegetables for a simple, frugal take on a classic dish.

1 (3–4 pound) cured corned beef, trimmed of fat

1½ cups water

½ teaspoon mustard seed

1 cinnamon stick

3 bay leaves

½ teaspoon whole allspice

½ teaspoon dill seeds

¼ teaspoon whole cloves

½ teaspoon peppercorns

1 head cabbage, cut into 6 wedges

4 medium carrots, peeled

3 medium onions, peeled and halved

6 medium red potatoes, peeled and halved

Preheat oven to 325°F. Place meat on rack in large Dutch oven. Add 1 cup water and spices. Cover and bake 3 hours. Partially cook cabbage, carrots, onions, and potatoes in boiling water until just barely tender; arrange around meat. Add ½ cup water; bake 1 hour, until vegetables are fully tender.

Part II: Big Dishes

Mediterranean-Style Beef-Stuffed Eggplant

price ($20)   servings (4)   price per serving ($5)

*T*his is a very inexpensive, filling dish that can work as a quick main course for dinner. It's hearty enough that you can serve it alone or alongside an easy steamed vegetable or mixed-green salad.

2 medium eggplants
1½ tablespoons olive oil
1 medium onion, chopped
1 pound ground beef
1 dash cinnamon
1 cup tomato sauce
Salt and pepper to taste
¼ cup pine nuts
¼ cup water

Cut eggplants in half lengthwise; scoop out center flesh. Set aside skins. Chop flesh into ½" pieces; sauté in pan with 1 tablespoon oil. Add onions; cook 5 minutes, until eggplant is soft. Add beef, cinnamon, ½ of tomato sauce, salt, and pepper; cook until beef is just browned, about 5 minutes. Stir pine nuts into beef mixture; set aside. Brush inside of eggplant skins with ½ tablespoon olive oil; place face up in shallow pan. Broil 10 minutes, until lightly brown, then turn oven to 375°F. Cook 5 minutes, until eggplant is soft. Spoon mixture back into eggplant halves. Dilute remaining tomato sauce with water; pour over eggplant halves and bake 30 minutes.

Spicy Beef and Black Bean Burritos

price $16   servings 8   price per serving $2

*T*hese burritos are brimming with ingredients, spices, and flavors, but luckily they're all extremely inexpensive and easy to find. Because these burritos are easily customizable, they're great to make for a crowd.

½ pound ground round chuck
¼ cup onion, chopped
¼ cup green bell pepper, chopped
1 tablespoon olive oil
1 (14-ounce) can diced tomatoes
2 teaspoons chili powder
½ teaspoon red pepper flakes
½ teaspoon oregano
½ teaspoon garlic powder
½ teaspoon salt
1 tablespoon fresh parsley, chopped
1 (15-ounce) can black beans, drained
8 flour tortillas
1½ cups Cheddar cheese, shredded
2 cups lettuce, shredded
Salsa (optional)

In a large skillet, brown beef with onion and green pepper in 1 tablespoon olive oil. Add tomatoes, chili powder, red pepper, oregano, garlic powder, salt, and parsley. Simmer until mixture thickens, about 10 minutes. Add beans; stir and heat 3 more minutes. Heat tortillas; spread mixture into each tortilla. Top with cheese, lettuce, and salsa. Roll up burrito and serve.

PART II: BIG DISHES

SEAFOOD

Asian-Inspired Baked Cod

price　$20　servings　6　price per serving　$3.35

There are some ingredients that we can't resist throwing into every dish we create. Reading over our recipes, they seem to pop up everywhere: avocado, mint, lemon, ginger, and ponzu. Ponzu is a soy-like sauce with a hint of citrus. It's a great component for a marinade, and it transforms a simple fillet of cod into a sophisticated and flavorful dinner. Baked over carrots, this is ideal for a healthy weeknight meal.

2 tablespoons soy sauce

2 tablespoons ponzu sauce

2 tablespoons sesame oil

3 tablespoons water

2 teaspoons granulated sugar

⅛ teaspoon crushed red pepper

2 cloves garlic, minced

2" piece ginger, peeled and minced

4 carrots, sliced into matchsticks

2 pounds cod fillets

Preheat oven to 400°F. In a small bowl, whisk together soy sauce, ponzu, sesame oil, water, sugar, and red pepper; toss in garlic and ginger. Arrange carrots in shallow baking dish. Scoop garlic and ginger out of the marinade; toss with carrots. Arrange fish fillets on top of carrots; pour marinade over. Bake 20 minutes. Serve hot.

Chilean Sea Bass with Tomatoes and Wild Mushrooms

price $27   servings 4   price per serving $6.75

*H*ere's something to make for a special occasion. Wrapping the fish in foil before baking makes opening the dish feel like opening a present, and the delicious aroma that seeps out is itself a gift. We prefer mixed mushrooms, but you can use whatever is freshest or seasonal. Serve this alongside a simple salad of mixed greens for a sophisticated and delicate celebratory meal.

3 tablespoons olive oil

2 garlic cloves, very thinly sliced

¾ cup wild mushrooms

½ cup cherry tomatoes, halved

Salt and pepper to taste

2 tablespoons capers, drained

2 teaspoons fresh thyme, chopped

4 (6-ounce) fillets Chilean sea bass, 1" thick

1 whole lemon, thinly sliced

Preheat oven to 400°F. In heavy skillet, heat oil and sauté garlic 30 seconds. Add mushrooms, tomatoes, and salt and pepper; sauté until tomatoes are softened, about 1 minute. Stir in capers and thyme; remove from heat. Cut out 4 squares of aluminum foil 12–15" long; place in large shallow baking dish. Drizzle center of each square with a little olive oil; top with fish. Slide lemon slices under fish; top with mushroom and tomato mixture. Gather foil to form pouch; crimp closed, leaving no openings. Bake until just cooked through and flaky, 12–20 minutes, depending on thickness of fish. Transfer fillets and lemon slices to plates; spoon tomatoes, mushrooms, and juices over top. Serve immediately.

Better-than-Chesapeake Crab Cakes

price $25   servings 5   price per serving $5

*E*ven though Alanna is from Maryland, we adapted this recipe for crab cakes from a close family friend and foodie in New York. We serve them over salads for ourselves, but you can serve mini ones as appetizers or serve them on buns with tartar sauce for a substantial main dish. For a lighter tartar sauce substitute, just squeeze fresh lemon juice on top of your cakes.

> ¼ cup plus ½ cup unseasoned bread crumbs
>
> 2 dashes hot sauce
>
> 3 dashes Worcestershire sauce
>
> 2 tablespoons mayonnaise
>
> 1 tablespoon Dijon mustard
>
> 1 tablespoon coarsely chopped flat-leaf parsley
>
> 1 tablespoon grated carrot
>
> 1 tablespoon green pepper, finely diced
>
> 1 tablespoon red pepper, finely diced
>
> 1 medium shallot, diced and sautéed
>
> 2 tablespoons lemon juice, fresh squeezed
>
> ½ teaspoon celery flakes
>
> ¼ teaspoon Old Bay seasoning
>
> ¼ teaspoon dry mustard
>
> ¼ teaspoon coarse black pepper
>
> 1 egg, beaten
>
> 1 dash sea salt
>
> 1 pound lump crabmeat
>
> ¼ cup olive oil

Mix all ingredients in a large bowl except for crabmeat, ½ cup bread crumbs, and oil. Gently fold in crabmeat. Form into 6–10 cakes, about 2"–3" in diameter; dredge in remaining bread crumbs. Heat oil in pan until hot; fry cakes until golden brown on each side, about 4 minutes. Drain on paper towels and serve immediately.

Curried Tilapia and Sweet Potato Stew

price **$16**   servings **4**   price per serving **$4**

We use tilapia often because it's extremely versatile—thick enough to hold its own in a stew, flavorful enough to bake with just lemon, salt, and pepper, and mild enough to take on new flavors when well seasoned. Plus, it's wonderfully inexpensive. In this stew, tilapia is complemented by flavorful Asian flavors, but isn't overpowered. The dish comes together quickly and easily for a tasty weeknight meal.

2 tablespoons olive oil
1 medium onion, halved and thinly sliced
1 carrot, sliced
1½ tablespoons curry powder
1 tablespoon grated ginger
2 sweet potatoes, cut into 1" cubes
3 cups chicken stock
1½ cups light coconut milk
2 tablespoons chopped fresh basil
1 pound tilapia, cut into 1" chunks, seasoned with salt and pepper
Cilantro (optional, for garnish)

Heat oil in large pot. Add onion and carrot; sauté 3 minutes, until onion is soft. Add curry and ginger; sauté 1 minute. Add sweet potato, stock, coconut milk, and basil; simmer 15–20 minutes, until potatoes are soft. When potatoes are ready, add fish to top of soup; spoon a bit of liquid over it and let cook about 5 minutes, until cooked through. Spoon soup into bowls, garnish with cilantro, and serve.

Frugal Bouillabaisse

price $50   servings 10   price per serving $5

While many cooks are extremely particular about the components of their bouillabaisses, this is one soup that we find works with any number of variations or ingredients. As long as you integrate seafood, saffron, and white wine, we're convinced you can't go wrong.

½ cup olive oil

1 medium onion, chopped

3 leeks, whites only, sliced

2 cloves garlic, crushed

2 medium sweet red peppers, chopped

12-ounce can chopped tomatoes

4 stalks celery, thinly sliced

1 teaspoon fennel seed

¾ teaspoon dried thyme

2 bay leaves

3 whole cloves

Zest of 1 orange

3 pounds of 3 types of firm white-flesh fish (tilapia, catfish, cod, snapper, halibut, or haddock—whichever are least expensive)

6 cups vegetable broth

1 pound clams or mussels

1 pound cooked shrimp, shelled and deveined

½ teaspoon saffron

Salt and pepper to taste

2 tablespoons lemon juice

1½ cups white wine

Garlic croutons (optional)

Heat oil in a large pot; add onions, leeks, garlic, and red peppers. Sauté 2 minutes; add tomato, celery, fennel, thyme, bay leaf, cloves, and orange zest. Cook until onion is soft and golden. Cut fish into 2" pieces; add to vegetable mixture with broth. Bring to a boil; reduce and simmer uncovered 10 minutes. Add clams or mussels, shrimp, saffron, salt, pepper, lemon juice, and white wine. Bring to a gentle simmer; cook 10 minutes. Serve hot, topped with garlic croutons, if desired.

Halibut with Warm Mushrooms

price　$27　servings　4　price per serving　$6.75

*T*his dish is healthy and easy enough for a weeknight but more than impressive enough for guests. Stack the components neatly on a clean white plate for a stunningly minimalist presentation.

6 heads baby bok choy, leaves separated and washed

½ cup water

4 tablespoons soy sauce

4 tablespoons white wine

2 teaspoons fresh ginger, minced

2 pounds halibut, divided into 4 pieces

MUSHROOM SALAD:

4 tablespoons olive oil

6 cups mixed mushrooms (shitake, button, elephant ear), coarsely chopped

4 tablespoons white wine

½ cup soy sauce

6 tablespoons rice wine vinegar

1 teaspoon fresh ginger, minced

2 tablespoons chives, chopped very finely

4 tablespoons sugar

Juice of 1 lime

Immerse bok choy leaves in water; remove and transfer to large, preheated pan. Add ½ cup water; cover and reduce heat to low. Cook until tender, 4–5 minutes. Pour off liquid; return to low heat and stir in soy sauce, wine, and ginger. Place fish over bok choy; cook until opaque throughout, about 6 minutes. To make mushroom salad, heat olive oil in pan; add mushrooms. Cook 2 minutes; add wine and cook additional 3 minutes, until mushrooms soften. Whisk together soy sauce, vinegar, ginger, chives, sugar, and lime juice to make dressing. Combine mushrooms with dressing. Plate bok choy; top with halibut and mushroom salad.

Light Shrimp Summer Rolls

price $18   servings 4   price per serving $4.50

This is a great no-utensil summer meal that comes together in fewer than fifteen minutes. Because the dish is so simple, we highly recommend using the freshest, highest-quality ingredients you can find. Serve these with sea-salted edamame beans for a healthy, refreshing dinner.

12 rice paper wraps

½ pound cooked shrimp, shelled and deveined

3 carrots, shredded

1 pound vermicelli rice noodles, cooked according to package instructions

1 head romaine lettuce, cut in large pieces

1 cup fresh basil leaves

DIPPING SAUCE:

1 teaspoon sesame oil

3 teaspoons water

¼ cup peanut butter

3 teaspoons Dijon mustard (or substitute any other in your fridge)

1 teaspoon rice wine vinegar

2 teaspoons honey

Fill large bowl with warm water; dip rice paper wrap 5–10 seconds. Place wrap on cutting board; layer with 2–3 shrimp, carrots, rice noodles, lettuce, and top with basil leaves. Fold edges in, then roll up wraps so both sides are sealed. Repeat process until all wraps are rolled. Make dipping sauce by mixing ingredients together in small bowl. Serve with summer rolls at room temperature or slightly cooled.

Miso and Scallion Salmon Burgers

price $32   servings 8   price per serving $4

This recipe is for those who believe everything really does taste better on a bun but who are reluctant to scarf down meaty burgers on a regular basis. These are baked rather than pan cooked, and while you can dress them up with all of your favorite fixings, these boast such tasty Asian flavors that we'll sometimes just dig into them with a fork.

2 pounds salmon without skin
¼ cup miso paste
¼ cup green onions, chopped
½ cup panko (Japanese bread crumbs)
8 hamburger buns
1 avocado, sliced (for garnish)

Preheat oven to 400°F. Cut salmon into large pieces; place in food processor. Pulse several times until minced (you can also use a knife to cut salmon into very small pieces). In large bowl, mix salmon, miso paste, green onions, and panko; form into 8 patties about 4" in diameter. Place on oiled baking sheet; bake 12–15 minutes, or grill over high heat for about 3 minutes per side until salmon is cooked through Serve on buns with a few slices of avocado.

Lemon-Yogurt Salmon and Orzo Salad

price $20   servings 4   price per serving $5

When Alanna was younger, her family called orzo "rizzo" because she and her brothers couldn't pronounce the word properly. So while this recipe is actually for rizzo salad, we'll forgive those who prefer the mainstream title. We turn to this salad for spring and summer lunches or light dinners. Also, try grilling the fish instead of pan cooking it for a slightly stronger flavor.

1 medium yellow onion, sliced

1½ cups water

5 sprigs fresh dill, plus ⅔ cup chopped dill

½ teaspoon salt

½ teaspoon pepper

1 pound salmon, cut into fillets

1 box orzo or other small pasta

16 ounces plain yogurt

Juice of 2 lemons

Salt and pepper to taste

1 cucumber, peeled and thinly sliced

1 medium red bell pepper, chopped

½ medium red onion, diced

2 cups spinach leaves (optional)

Sauté onions 1 minute in pan with 1 tablespoon water. Add water, dill sprigs, salt, and pepper. Add salmon; cover pan and bring to a simmer. Simmer gently about 10 minutes, until salmon is cooked through. Remove from heat; cool and separate salmon into 1" chunks. Cook orzo according to package instructions. In a small bowl, combine yogurt, lemon juice, ⅔ cup dill, and salt and pepper to taste. Combine orzo, salmon, cucumber, red pepper, and onion in a large bowl. Toss with yogurt dressing. Serve alone or over spinach leaves.

Seared Tuna with Fennel

price $27 servings 4 price per serving $6.75

We love sushi, so when we make this salad we buy high-quality tuna and sear it just a touch. You can cook the fish to your liking, however, and it's sure to both look and taste incredible when surrounded by the elegant combination of spring vegetables and cool fennel in a light citrus dressing.

2 pounds tuna
Salt and pepper to taste
¼ pound fresh string beans
8 ounces mixed greens
2 bulbs small fennel, sliced very thinly
½ cup kalamata olives, pits removed

DRESSING:
½ cup olive oil
¼ cup freshly squeezed lemon juice
Salt and pepper to taste

Cut tuna into 4 pieces; salt and pepper each piece on both sides. Preheat grill; cook tuna to your taste (about 3 minutes on each side should cook it to rare). Blanch green beans by placing in boiling water 3 minutes, then removing and rinsing. Arrange greens on 4 plates; divide green beans, fennel, and olives among plates. Let tuna rest 5 minutes; slice and divide among plates. Whisk together dressing ingredients; pour over salad.

Shrimp Kind-of-Scampi

price $16   servings 4   price per serving $4

It's true—this is not shrimp scampi. It's loosely based on shrimp scampi, but healthier, lighter, and fresher. Feel free to use as much lemon as you can handle.

1 pound shrimp, peeled and deveined
5 garlic cloves, minced
1 cup bread crumbs

Juice of 1 lemon
1 pound fresh mushrooms, sliced
3 tablespoons butter

Preheat oven to 400°F. Combine everything but butter in ovenproof dish. Cut butter into small pieces; scatter on top. Bake 20 minutes, or until shrimp are cooked. Serve plain or over pasta.

Spicy Grilled Shrimp

price $15   servings 5   price per serving $3

This delicious shrimp dish is simple, frugal, and packed with flavor! Try it for dinner, served over rice or steamed vegetables.

¼ cup olive oil
¼ cup gin
2 garlic cloves, mashed
2 pounds uncooked shrimp

1 teaspoon salt
½ teaspoon Tabasco sauce
½ cup chili sauce
20 wooden skewers

Combine ingredients in dish; allow shrimp to marinate 1 hour in refrigerator. Soak wooden skewers in water. Thread about 4 shrimp on wet skewers; grill 2–3 minutes on each side. Serve skewered shrimp as appetizers or remove from skewers and serve over rice as main dish.

Soy-Braised Salmon Steaks

price $20   servings 4   price per serving $5

*T*here's food that we cook, and there's food that we live on. We cook paella and cupcakes and apple butternut squash soup. We live on turkey wraps and salads and fruit. This recipe represents food we both cook and live on. It's healthy and easy, with all of our favorite flavors. Vegetables are already incorporated, so just serve it alongside brown rice or a sweet potato.

2 tablespoons vegetable oil
4 salmon steaks, ½ pound each
Salt and pepper to taste
3 leeks, whites only, sliced
3 medium carrots, sliced in rounds
3" piece ginger, peeled and sliced
1 cup sake or dry cooking wine
3 tablespoons mirin
3 tablespoons soy sauce
1 tablespoon sugar

Heat oil in heavy skillet on medium-high heat. Season salmon with salt and pepper; add to pan. Sear on both sides until golden; remove and set aside. Add leeks, carrots, and ginger to pan; sauté until just soft. Combine sake, mirin, soy sauce, and sugar in a small bowl; add to pan to deglaze. Put salmon back in pan; cover and cook until done, about 10–15 minutes depending on thickness of salmon. Serve hot with vegetables and sauce from pan.

Thyme-Encrusted Salmon

price $24   servings 4   price per serving $6

Some things pair well—pancakes and Sundays, coffee and biscotti—but other things, when combined, absolutely sing. You wouldn't expect a duo as simple as salmon and mashed potatoes to fall into this group, but here, flavorful herbed salmon accompanies classic potatoes so harmoniously that we can't imagine them apart. The drizzled balsamic reduction sweeps the entire dish together for a meal so sweet you'll beg for an encore.

2 tablespoons dried thyme
Salt and pepper to taste
1½-pound salmon fillet, cut into 4 pieces
3 tablespoons olive oil
1 cup balsamic vinegar
1 teaspoon sugar

MASHED POTATOES:
2 pounds red potatoes, washed and cut into 2" pieces
3 tablespoons butter
¾ cup milk
1 garlic clove, crushed
Salt and pepper to taste

Combine thyme, salt, and pepper in dish. Brush salmon with olive oil; press into thyme mixture. Heat olive oil in large skillet on medium heat; place salmon flesh-side down. Cook 2 minutes, flip to skin side. Cook additional 5–7 minutes, until done; set aside. Bring 1 cup balsamic vinegar and sugar to boil in small saucepan; reduce to ⅓ cup. For mashed potatoes, boil potatoes in medium pot of salted water until tender. Drain in colander; mash in large mixing bowl. Add butter, milk, garlic, salt, and pepper. Serve salmon over mashed potatoes; drizzle with balsamic vinegar reduction.

PART II: BIG DISHES
VEGETARIAN

Chickpea and Broccoli Orecchiette

price $16   servings 4   price per serving  $4

We prefer pasta dishes that are light and fresh rather than those heavily bogged down with sauce and meat. This quick pasta number will leave you feeling satisfied but not stuffed. It's even light enough for summer, when freshly picked tomatoes will elevate the dish to something heavenly.

> 1 head broccoli, cut into small florets
> 2 tablespoons olive oil
> 1 small red onion, diced
> 2 tablespoons garlic, chopped
> 12 ounce can chickpeas (garbanzo beans), cooked
> ½ pound orecchiette or other shaped pasta, cooked
> 2 cups fresh plum tomatoes, chopped
> Salt and pepper to taste
> Parmesan cheese, freshly grated (optional)

Place broccoli in shallow pan with 1" water; cook covered until tender, about 3 minutes. Heat olive oil in pan; sauté onion and garlic until onions begin to soften, about 2 minutes. Toss in chickpeas, broccoli, orecchiette, and tomatoes; cook additional 3 minutes. Add salt and pepper and top with freshly grated Parmesan.

Chilled Peanut Butter Noodles

price $12   servings 8   price per serving $1.50

No matter how badly you want to devour these noodles in your first sitting, try to save some for the next day. The peanut sauce will have thickened, and the noodles will be colder, chewier, and more delicious. This recipe calls for regular spaghetti and just a few fresh vegetables to lighten it up and add a refreshing crunch.

4 ounces shitake mushrooms, thinly sliced

1 pound spaghetti noodles, cooked and cooled

1 cucumber, peeled, halved lengthwise and thinly sliced

4 scallions, thinly sliced

1 medium red pepper, thinly sliced

SAUCE:

6 tablespoons peanut butter

6 tablespoons soy sauce

3 teaspoons sesame oil

1 tablespoon ground ginger

½ cup water

Simmer mushrooms in a shallow pan with about 1" of water for about 4 minutes, until mushrooms are soft, then drain (or steam them in a microwave-safe bowl with some water for 1 minute). Put pasta in large bowl; add cucumber, scallion, red pepper, and mushrooms. In small bowl, combine peanut butter, soy sauce, sesame oil, ginger, and water. Toss with noodle mixture and serve at room temperature.

Colorful Risotto-Stuffed Peppers

price $12   servings 4   price per serving $3

This dish is as gorgeous as it is delicious. Because we chop up a little bit of each colored pepper to toss into the risotto filling, the peppers appear as though they have been stuffed with confetti. They're also deceivingly filling, so this dish may be sufficient on its own for lunch or a smaller dinner.

1 medium green bell pepper
1 medium orange bell pepper
1 medium red bell pepper
1 medium, yellow bell pepper
2 tablespoons olive oil
1 medium red onion, chopped
1 large portobello mushroom, cut into ½" pieces
1 cup arborio rice
3 cups chicken broth
½ cup freshly grated Parmesan cheese, plus some additional

Cut off top ¼ of each pepper; remove stems and dice tops. Heat oil in a large pan; add diced pepper tops and onions. Cook 4–5 minutes, or until peppers are soft; add mushrooms and cook additional 2 minutes. Add rice, cook 1 minute; add 1 cup chicken broth. Gradually add remaining 2 cups chicken broth over 10 minutes, stirring continually. Stir in cheese. Cook risotto 20 minutes, until most of liquid has been absorbed. Preheat oven to 350°F. Divide risotto among peppers; top with sprinkling of Parmesan. Bake 30 minutes, until outside shell is soft.

Eggplant Pasta alla Siciliana

price $16   servings 8   price per serving $2

We begged Alanna's close family friend to lend us this recipe for our cookbook, since it is among the best pasta dishes we've ever tasted. Although it's vegetarian, the eggplant sauce is hearty, with the currants and pine nuts adding flavor and texture. Even when our friend would bring enormous bowls over for potlucks, there wasn't a chance this Italian masterpiece would last the night.

¼ cup olive oil

2 medium eggplants, peeled and diced

1 large onion, diced

3 cloves garlic, minced

Salt and pepper to taste

2 teaspoons oregano

¾ cup red wine

1 (28-ounce) can diced tomatoes

¾ cup currants or golden raisins

¼ cup pine nuts, toasted

1 pound farfalle pasta

Heat olive oil in deep skillet or large pot; add eggplant. Let one side of eggplant brown over medium heat 8 minutes, turn to brown other side. Add onion, garlic, salt, and pepper; cook additional 10 minutes. Add oregano and wine; cook 10 minutes. Add canned tomatoes; cook covered 30 minutes. Add currants or raisins and pine nuts. Lower heat; cook 5 more minutes. Cook pasta according to package directions until al dente; drain and place in large bowl. Spoon sauce over pasta and serve.

Farfalle with Portobello Mushrooms

price $15   servings 5   price per serving $3

This is an easy meatless dish that we always recommend to friends and aspiring chefs because it's easy and frugal. It's also easy on the eyes, with a sprinkling of shaved Parmesan and a parsley, and the portobellos make a great and filling alternative to meat.

2 tablespoons olive oil

2 medium onions, finely diced

4 medium portobello mushrooms, sliced and cut into 2" pieces

1 clove garlic

2 tablespoons tomato paste

½ cup red wine

3 teaspoons fresh rosemary

Salt and pepper to taste

1 pound farfalle pasta, cooked

1 tablespoon parsley (dried or finely chopped fresh)

Parmesan cheese (for garnish)

Heat olive oil in large pan; add onions and cook until soft, 2–3 minutes. Add portobellos and garlic; cook 5 minutes. Add tomato paste, wine, and rosemary; cook 5 more minutes, until mushrooms are cooked. Add salt and pepper. Add cooked pasta to pan and toss with mushrooms. Top with parsley, garnish with cheese, and serve.

Gorgonzola Pizza with Radicchio and Asian Pears

price $12   servings 4   price per serving $3

This is another of our very favorite recipes. We love to combine Gorgonzola, radicchio, and pears in salads, and we blew our own minds when we discovered that we could combine them in pizza form as well. Asian pears are an incredibly unique and tasty fruit—we think they look and taste like the perfect hybrid of apple and pear, but if you can't find them cheap, feel free to substitute other varieties of pear.

1 Homemade Pizza Crust (see recipe page 136)
2 tablespoons olive oil
6 ounces Gorgonzola cheese, crumbled
½ head radicchio, coarsely chopped
1 Asian pear, cut into 1" slices
1 tablespoon fresh rosemary, chopped

Preheat oven to 500°F and heat up pizza stone. On flour-dusted baking sheet or countertop, roll out pizza dough to desired thickness. Brush dough with olive oil. Cover crust with Gorgonzola cheese, radicchio, Asian pear, and rosemary. Transfer to heated pizza stone. Bake 20 minutes and serve hot.

Israeli Couscous Salad

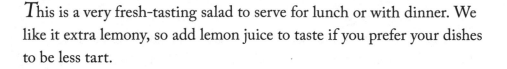

price $8   servings 6   price per serving $1.35

*T*his is a very fresh-tasting salad to serve for lunch or with dinner. We like it extra lemony, so add lemon juice to taste if you prefer your dishes to be less tart.

2 cups dry Israeli couscous
1 cucumber, peeled and chopped
1 medium red pepper, chopped
1 medium orange pepper, chopped
3 scallions, chopped
1 tablespoon fresh flat-leaf parsley, chopped
1 tablespoon fresh dill, chopped
2 tablespoons olive oil
Juice of 1–2 lemons
Salt and pepper to taste

Cook couscous according to package instructions. In a bowl, combine couscous with cucumber, peppers, scallions, parsley, and dill. Toss with olive oil and lemon juice and season to taste with salt and pepper.

Mediterranean Salad with Lentils, Tomato, and Feta

price $8   servings 4   price per serving $2

This salad can be as easy as you want it to be. Buy precooked lentils for a less-than-five-minute assembly, or soak and cook them from scratch. You can scoop the salad into intact romaine leaves or eat the lentils straight from the bowl. Any way you serve it this dish is flavorful and tasty, especially with fresh summer mint.

4 cups lentils
2 cup cherry tomatoes, halved
1 cup mint, chopped
½ cup olive oil
6 tablespoons red wine vinegar
12 ounces crumbled feta
Salt and pepper to taste
Romaine leaves (optional)

Cook lentils according to package instructions; drain and pat dry with paper towels. Let cool. Combine lentils, tomatoes, and mint in a bowl. In a separate bowl, whisk together oil and vinegar; pour over lentils. Add feta, salt, and pepper. Serve in individual romaine leaves.

Moroccan-Style Veggie Stew

price $16   servings 8   price per serving $2

In the depths of winter, when the only seasonal items are root vegetables and onions, break out this recipe for a spicy, tasty stew that will warm you over until spring.

3 tablespoons olive oil

2 medium yellow onions, chopped

2 garlic cloves, minced

2 tablespoons curry powder

1½ tablespoons ground cumin

1 teaspoon cinnamon

½ teaspoon cayenne pepper

2 sweet potatoes, cut into ½" pieces

2 parsnips, cut into ½" pieces

2 turnips, cut into ½" pieces

4 carrots, cut into 1" pieces

4 cups chicken or vegetable stock

1 head cauliflower, cut into 1" florets

1 (16-ounce) can chickpeas, drained

1 (16-ounce) can diced tomatoes

Salt and pepper to taste

2 cups couscous, cooked according to package

¼ cup fresh cilantro, chopped

1 cup peanuts, chopped

In a large pot, heat oil on medium-high heat. Add onions; cook 3–4 minutes, until just soft. Add garlic, curry powder, cumin, cinnamon, and cayenne; continue to cook 30 seconds. Add sweet potatoes, parsnips, turnips, carrots, and broth. Bring to a simmer; add cauliflower, chickpeas and canned tomatoes. Simmer 20–30 minutes, until vegetables are soft. Season with salt and pepper. Serve over couscous and top with cilantro and sprinkling of chopped peanuts.

Mushroom and Leek Pizza

price ⬤ $7   servings ⬤ 4   price per serving ⬤ $3.50

This is an upscale take on mushroom and onion pizza—all the classic flavors are there, but leeks make this version a bit more unique and complex. Button mushrooms are our default for this dish, but we're always experimenting with other varieties as well.

1½ cups leeks, sliced

2 garlic cloves, crushed

3 tablespoons olive oil

1½ cups white mushrooms, sliced

Salt and pepper to taste

1 Homemade Pizza Crust (see recipe page 136)

½ cup tomato sauce

8 ounces mozzarella cheese, shredded

Preheat oven to 500°F. In large pan, sauté leeks and garlic in 1 tablespoon olive oil 3 minutes. Add mushrooms; cook 3 minutes, adding salt and pepper to taste. Roll out pizza dough to desired thickness; place on flour-dusted baking sheet or heated pizza stone. Brush with remaining olive oil. Spread tomato sauce over dough, leaving 1" around edges. Sprinkle on cheese and top with mushroom and leek mixture. Bake 10–15 minutes, until lightly brown. Serve hot.

Mushroom and Rosemary Marinara

price $8   servings 5 price per serving $1.60

There are infinite recipes for marinara sauce floating around, but we stick with this one because it is inexpensive, comprehensive, and classic.

¼ cup olive oil

1 medium onion, minced

2 garlic cloves, minced

5 ounces white mushrooms, sliced

2 tablespoons fresh rosemary

2 (28-ounce) cans tomatoes, crushed or diced

Salt and pepper to taste

1 teaspoon dried oregano

2 teaspoons honey

Heat oil in large saucepan over medium heat. Sauté onions until soft. Add garlic, mushrooms, and rosemary. Stir in tomatoes, salt, pepper, oregano, and honey. Bring to a boil; reduce heat and simmer 40–50 minutes. Serve over pasta.

Orange-Flavored Tofu

price $6   servings 4   price per serving $1.50

*P*eople complain about tofu being flavorless, but this orange tofu has taste: it's sweet, orangey, savory, and delicious. It's even a bit crunchy around the edges. It goes wonderfully over Toasted Coconut Rice (page 146) or you can try it over greens in an Asian-inspired salad.

2 blocks firm tofu
¼ cup orange juice
¼ cup sherry
2 tablespoons sesame oil
¼ cup brown sugar
2 tablespoons ground ginger
4 tablespoons soy sauce
1 teaspoon orange zest

Drain tofu. Slice each block into thirds; press tofu by placing slices in between thick layers of paper towels (about 3 three sheets per layer). Place heavy item like baking dish with water on top of tofu. Press tofu 2 hours, changing paper towels after 1 hour to eliminate excess liquid. Meanwhile, whisk together orange juice, sherry, soy sauce, brown sugar, ground ginger, sesame oil, and lemon zest. Place tofu in baking dish; pour marinade over, turning to make sure marinade is on both sides. Marinate 30 minutes. Preheat oven to 375°F. Bake, covered with aluminum foil, 20 minutes, then without foil additional 15 minutes. Turn on broiler; broil additional 5–7 minutes, until browned. Serve over Toasted Coconut Rice (see recipe page 146).

Homemade Pizza Crust

price $4   servings 4   price per serving $1

This is our go-to recipe for a medium-thickness pizza crust. It's simple and easy and hasn't failed us yet.

4½ cups flour (all-purpose or high-gluten)
2 teaspoons instant dry yeast
2 teaspoons salt
2 tablespoons sugar
2 tablespoons olive oil
1¾ cups cold water

In large bowl, food processor, or standing mixer, combine 4 cups flour, yeast, salt, and sugar. Add olive oil and water; stir together until mixture becomes dough. Knead 10 minutes, or until elastic, adding more flour as needed to keep it from sticking. Form into 2 large balls; place in 2 lightly oiled bowls. Cover and set aside to rise 1–2 hours. When doubled in size, punch down; let rest 20 minutes. To make pizza, roll dough out on floured surface or toss to form a large flat disk. Pizza dough will keep in refrigerator for up to 6 days.

Quinoa Risotto with Wild Mushrooms

price $15   servings 5   price per serving $3

We love to cook with quinoa because it's so incredibly healthy. Admittedly, turning it into a risotto isn't the healthiest route we could take with this tasty ingredient because it adds butter and oil, but we think it's worth it for the flavor-packed result. Using homemade broth is key in this recipe, as it holds the entire dish together.

2 cups quinoa
2 tablespoons olive oil
2 tablespoons butter
1 pound wild mushrooms, chopped
1 medium yellow onion, diced
1 large shallot, diced
4 cups chicken stock, hot
2 teaspoons fresh thyme (or 1 teaspoon dried)
½ cup Parmesan cheese, freshly grated, plus more for garnish
Salt and pepper to taste

Rinse quinoa in fine mesh strainer; drain well and set aside. In large skillet, heat 1 tablespoon olive oil and 1 tablespoon butter over medium-high heat. Add mushrooms; cook 8 minutes, or until brown and tender. Remove from pan and set aside. In same skillet, heat remaining olive oil and butter. Add onions and shallots; cook 2–3 minutes, until just soft. Add quinoa; cook 2 minutes, until warmed. Add stock; bring to a boil. Reduce heat; simmer and cook until liquid is reduced and quinoa is softened, about 15–20 minutes. Return mushrooms to pan with thyme and Parmesan cheese; cook until cheese is melted and mushrooms are fully cooked. Adjust seasoning to taste and garnish with freshly grated Parmesan cheese. Serve warm.

Quinoa-Stuffed Summer Squash

price $18   servings 6   price per serving $3

We first made this dish with gorgeous summer squash from a small roadside farm stand in Maine. The vegetables are stunning to begin with, but they are even more beautiful when overflowing with a flavorful and healthy grain like quinoa. The cumin and Gouda lend the dish a surprising smoky flavor.

6 medium round summer squash
2 tablespoons olive oil
1 medium onion, chopped
1 medium red bell pepper, chopped
1 cup white mushrooms, sliced thinly and halved
¼ cup red wine
2 cups quinoa, cooked according to package instructions
½ teaspoon cumin
Salt and pepper to taste
½ cup smoked Gouda cheese, grated (optional)

Preheat oven to 350°F. Carefully cut along top edge of squash; remove top with stem. If cavity is not large enough to stuff, scoop out squash flesh. Place squash in baking dish; bake 40 minutes, until insides have softened. Heat olive oil in large pan; add onions and cook until soft, about 3 minutes. Add pepper and squash flesh; cook 1–2 minutes. Add mushrooms and wine; cook until all vegetables are cooked, about 2 minutes. In large bowl, gently stir together vegetable mixture and quinoa; add cumin, salt, and pepper. Spoon into squash and top with cheese; bake 10 minutes, until cheese is melted and squash is soft. Remove from oven; mix quinoa and cheese together if desired inside squash.

Ratatouille Niçoise

price $20   servings 8   price per serving $2.50

This recipe requires some chopping, but once everything is prepped it's quick and easy. The flavors are familiar and rustic, and you should have no trouble finding nearly all the ingredients locally if you set out to make this during late summer or early fall.

½ cup olive oil
1 large onion, chopped
4 cloves garlic, minced
1 medium eggplant, peeled and cut into small cubes
2 medium green peppers, chopped
4 small zucchini, chopped
2 bay leaves, crumbled
1 teaspoon dried thyme
1 teaspoon salt
½ teaspoon black pepper
⅛ teaspoon hot pepper flakes
2 (28-ounce) cans chopped tomatoes
1 cup pitted Kalamata olives, cut in half
1 cup pitted green olives, cut in half
½ cup Italian parsley, chopped
1 cup Parmesan cheese, freshly grated

Heat olive oil in large pot. Sauté onions and garlic 3 minutes. Add eggplant; cook 5 minutes. Add peppers, zucchini, and spices; cook 5 minutes. Add tomatoes; bring to a boil. Add olives and parsley. Cover and cook 10 minutes. Serve warm with fresh Parmesan cheese.

Roasted Summer Veggie Lasagna

price $20   servings 8   price per serving $2.50

*O*nce upon a time, we carefully measured the ratio of vegetables to cheese, and made sure we placed the layers in order. Now we realize there's no way to mess this up, and we add any vegetables we have in the fridge. This dish freezes well and tastes fantastic with every reheat.

2 medium zucchini, sliced thinly (1 yellow, 1 green)

1 medium tomato, sliced thinly

2 portabello mushrooms, sliced thinly

2 peppers, sliced

1 onion, sliced thinly

1 eggplant, sliced thinly

½ cup olive oil

⅓ cup balsamic vinegar

Salt and pepper to taste

1 box whole-wheat lasagna pasta

⅓ cup pesto (store-bought or homemade, see recipe page 50)

2 cups part-skim ricotta cheese

2½ cups mozzarella cheese, shredded

½ cup Parmesan cheese, grated

1 16-ounce jar tomato sauce

Preheat oven to 350°F. Line baking sheets with parchment paper. Toss vegetables in oil and vinegar; sprinkle with salt and pepper. Spread on baking sheets; roast 30 minutes, or until caramelized. Cook pasta until just barely done; mix pesto and ricotta together in bowl. In another bowl, combine mozzarella and Parmesan. When vegetables are done, turn oven to 325°F. Layer lasagna in 9" × 13" baking dish by adding sauce to bottom, then 3 noodles, ⅓ of pesto-ricotta mixture, ⅓ of vegetable mixture, then ¼ of mozzarella-Parmesan mixture. Repeat twice, then add remaining mozzarella-Parmesan and any leftover vegetables or sauce to top. Bake 40 minutes uncovered; let sit 10 minutes before serving. Freeze single portions in plastic containers for up to 6 months for easy weeknight meals.

Spaghetti Squash with Pesto

price $16   servings 4   price per serving $4

*S*paghetti squash is the ultimate carbohydrate imposter. Like pasta, it tastes like whatever you dress it in. Because we love pesto, it's an obvious choice for us. We prefer the pesto fresh, but if a store-bought version is more convenient, it's a forgivable substitute.

2 medium spaghetti squash
¼ cup Basil Pesto (see recipe page 50)
½ cup Parmesan cheese, freshly grated

Preheat oven to 350°F. Halve each squash; place face down on greased baking sheet. Bake 30 minutes, until tender. After squash has cooked and cooled slightly, remove seeds from middle; use fork to scrape out flesh—it should come out in spaghetti-like strips. Toss squash and pesto together, topped with Parmesan cheese. Serve warm.

Japanese Eggplant with Peanut Soy Sauce

price 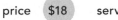 $18   servings 6   price per serving $3

When Alanna's best childhood friend came home from winter break during her postgraduate year in Japan, she brought this recipe with her. It's just sweet enough and has the perfect amount of spice and salt. While Japanese eggplants work well, we use whatever we can find inexpensively at the farmer's market or grocery store.

2 eggplants, cut lengthwise into 1½" thick slices
3 tablespoons peanut butter
1½ tablespoons soy sauce
1½ tablespoons sake or dry white wine
½ tablespoon sugar
⅛ teaspoon chili powder

Steam eggplant slices in microwave 2–3 minutes, or over small amount of boiling water. When tender, quickly rinse under cold water to prevent discoloration. In small saucepan, combine peanut butter, soy sauce, sake or wine, sugar, and chili powder. Simmer on medium heat 5 minutes, stirring constantly, until smooth. Spoon sauce over eggplant slices and serve warm.

Sweet and Sour Veggies over Rice

price $18   servings 6   price per serving $3

When we crave the flavors of Chinese food, we'll whip up this mock-Chinese dish. It contains all of the flavors with none of the fat—just steamed vegetables in a syrupy sweet and sour sauce over perfectly cooked white rice.

½ head napa cabbage, cut into 2" pieces
3 carrots, sliced
2 cups snow peas
2 cups shitake mushrooms, sliced
1 head broccoli, cut into 2" pieces
6 eggs
2 cups rice, cooked according to package directions
2 tablespoons soy sauce
¼ cup sweet and sour sauce
1 teaspoon Sriracha hot sauce
2 green onions, sliced
1 cup bean sprouts

In a large pot, steam cabbage, carrots, snow peas, mushrooms, and broccoli 6–8 minutes, until vegetables are tender. In a skillet, fry each egg over easy and set aside. Divide rice into bowls; spoon vegetables over rice and top with fried egg. Mix together soy sauce, sweet and sour sauce, and Sriracha sauce in small bowl; spoon sauce over rice and vegetables. Top with green onions and bean sprouts. Serve warm.

White Pizza with Spinach and Artichoke Hearts

price $16   servings 4   price per serving $4

This pizza is our attempt to recreate Alanna's favorite pizza from a pizzeria in her hometown. If you don't want to buy roasted artichoke hearts, you can steam and roast your own.

2 medium Homemade Pizza Crusts (see recipe page 136)

2 tablespoons olive oil

8 ounces mozzarella cheese, shredded

9 ounces spinach, steamed and chopped

1 tomato, thinly sliced

1 jar roasted artichoke hearts, drained and sliced

1 teaspoon dried oregano

1 teaspoon fresh thyme

Salt and pepper to taste

Preheat oven to 500°F. On flour-dusted baking sheet or heated pizza stone, roll out pizza dough to desired thickness. Brush dough with olive oil. Cover crust with mozzarella, spinach, tomato, and artichokes. Sprinkle with oregano, thyme, salt, and pepper. Bake 10–15 minutes. Serve hot.

PART II: BIG DISHES
SiDE DiSHES

Asian Green Bean Salad

price $12   servings 4   price per serving $3

This is a recipe that Alanna invented on the spot for a picnic, and it quickly entered the regular rotation of recipes. The tartness of the tomatoes cuts the sweetness of the sauce, and you can throw in other vegetables like cucumbers or peppers as well.

1 pound string beans, trimmed and steamed   ¼ cup soy sauce

1 pint cherry tomatoes, halved   ¼ cup hot water

½ cup peanut butter   2 tablespoons honey

In large bowl, combine string beans and cherry tomatoes. In small bowl, whisk together peanut butter, soy sauce, hot water, and honey. Toss vegetables with dressing until coated.

Toasted Coconut Rice

price $6   servings 4   price per serving $1.50

This recipe produces amazing results for almost no effort, and it's a great way to get the flavor of coconut rice without the weight of coconut milk or butter. We serve it as a side to numerous main courses, and always head back to the refrigerator to pick at leftovers for a late-night snack.

2 cups white basmati rice   3 tablespoons ginger, grated

2 cups unsweetened coconut flakes, toasted   ½ teaspoon lemongrass, dried

Cook rice according to package instructions. Gently toss in coconut, ginger, and lemongrass. Serve hot.

Baked Yucca Fries

price $6   servings 4   price per serving $1.50

*I*n this recipe, we cut yucca into fry-sized wedges and roast them. There's no grease and hardly any fat—just the sweet yucca, with a hint of garlic and salt.

2 pounds fresh yucca, peeled and cut crosswise into 3" sections
1 tablespoon olive oil   1 teaspoon kosher salt
2 garlic cloves, crushed   1 teaspoon fresh pepper

Preheat oven to 400°F. Place yucca in large pot; cover with water. Bring to a boil; lower heat and simmer 15–30 minutes, until just tender. Cut slices into ½" wedges. Toss with olive oil, garlic, salt, and pepper. Bake on nonstick baking sheet 30 minutes, turning every 10 minutes, until browned.

Roasted Cauliflower with Marjoram

price $4   servings 4   price per serving $1

*W*e included a recipe for roasted cauliflower in our very first blog post. We roasted bucketfuls to bring to a picnic in Philly and ate it like popcorn. This recipe is a staple for us, and one that even the most vegetable-adverse will adore.

1 head cauliflower   1 teaspoon pepper
⅓ cup olive oil   2 teaspoons dried marjoram
2 teaspoons kosher salt

Preheat oven to 400°F. Cut cauliflower into individual florets. In large bowl, toss cauliflower, olive oil, salt, pepper, and marjoram. Arrange in single layer on baking sheet. Bake 25 minutes, turning once, until cauliflower is lightly browned and slightly crispy.

Balsamic Grilled Artichokes

price **$18**　servings **6**　price per serving **$3**

We believe this is the best way to prepare artichokes, and we use this recipe all the time when artichokes are in season. The natural sweetness of the artichokes is balanced perfectly by the punchy cayenne aioli. You can use baby artichokes and serve them as appetizers, but we usually buy the biggest artichokes available because we can't get enough of the great smoky flavors in this dish.

6 artichokes

½ cup olive oil

¼ cup balsamic vinegar

2 tablespoons Italian seasonings (or a mixture of dried oregano and fennel seeds)

2 teaspoons sugar

½ teaspoon salt

½ teaspoon pepper

AIOLI:

¼ cup mayonnaise

2 teaspoons cayenne

1 clove garlic, crushed

Wash artichokes and clip off sharp tips of leaves with scissors. Boil in large pot of water, covered, 20–25 minutes, until leaves are soft enough to pluck easily. Remove from water and let cool. Whisk together oil, vinegar, seasonings, sugar, salt, and pepper. Once artichokes are cool, cut in half and divide between 2 large zip-top bags. Divide vinaigrette between bags; marinate at least 1 hour. Preheat grill to high; cook artichokes (reserve marinade) 3–5 minutes on each side, until slightly crispy. Pour extra marinade into bowl; combine with mayonnaise, cayenne, and garlic. Taste and adjust seasonings.

Festive Ravioli Salad

price $20   servings 12   price per serving $1.65

We used to roll our eyes at the mention of pasta salads, mentally grouping them in the category "Lame Potluck Dishes of the '90s." But after making one as a side for a large New Year's Eve party one year, we now sing a different tune. This pasta salad is *anything* but lame and bland—it boasts a wide range of flavors and textures, with a tangy vinaigrette that enhances the flavors.

1 bunch asparagus, cut into 1"–2" pieces
½ cup olive oil
Salt and pepper to taste
3 pounds cheese ravioli, cooked
½ head radicchio, shredded
½ cup sun-dried tomatoes, chopped
½ cup kalamata olives, pitted and chopped
½ cup yellow pepper, thinly sliced
¼ cup balsamic vinegar
½ cup fresh basil, chopped

Preheat oven to 350°F. Toss asparagus with 2 tablespoons olive oil, salt, and pepper; roast 20 minutes. Remove from oven and add to ravioli. Add radicchio, sun-dried tomatoes, olives, and pepper; toss to combine. In separate bowl, whisk together remaining olive oil, vinegar, basil, and salt and pepper to taste. Dress salad and serve at room temperature.

Fresh-Baked Bread

price **$5**   servings **5**   price per serving **$1**

This French bread recipe takes an afternoon to complete, but for just a few hours of effort, you can make fresh bread crumbs, croutons for a salad, a vehicle for mopping up gravy, or even sandwich bread for lunch or dinner. Given the low cost and easy effort (most of the "cooking" time is spent letting the bread rise), we think soft and rustic homemade bread is definitely worth it.

3½ cups all-purpose flour
2 teaspoons salt
1 teaspoon instant yeast
Scant 1½ cups warm water
1 tablespoon olive oil

Combine flour, salt, and yeast in food processor; process 5 seconds. Slowly pour water in while machine is running. Process about 30 seconds, until dough forms a shaggy ball. Transfer to large bowl; cover with plastic wrap and let rise 3 hours. Divide into 3 balls; let rise, covered, 30 minutes. Sprinkle a little flour on counter; flatten each ball into 8" × 10" rectangle and fold short ends to middle, sealing seam. Spread towel on counter; place on towel, seam-side down. Let rise another 1–2 hours. Preheat oven to 450°F; make cut along top of each loaf with sharp knife. Brush with olive oil; bake on lightly floured baking sheet 25–35 minutes, until crust is golden brown.

Mashed Asian Sweet Potatoes

price $8   servings 4   price per serving $2

White sweet potatoes are an obsession. We like to consider ourselves white sweet potato elves, searching for this unique ingredient in Asian grocery stores and farmers' markets and sharing it with everyone we meet. Whenever we encounter someone who hasn't tasted them, we can't resist whipping up a dish like this one to highlight this sweet ingredient. It goes wonderfully as a side to the Asian-Inspired Baked Cod (see recipe page 110). If you can't find white sweet potatoes, it is possible to substitute regular sweet potatoes for a similar result.

3 white sweet potatoes, peeled
1 tablespoon butter
3 tablespoons ponzu sauce (an Japanese citrus-based sauce)
2 tablespoons brown sugar
1 teaspoon ground ginger
1 teaspoon fresh ginger, grated
Salt and pepper to taste

Bring large pot of water to boil. Cut sweet potatoes into large chunks. Add to boiling water; boil 30 minutes, until soft. Drain and put in large bowl; mash until soft. Add butter, ponzu, brown sugar, ground ginger, and fresh ginger; continue mashing. Season with salt and pepper.

Potato Salad with Fresh Herbs

price $12   servings 8   price per serving $1.50

This salad is inspired by our favorite method for roasting potatoes—with rosemary, thyme, a dash of olive oil, salt, and pepper. We both crave potato salads as a summery side dish, and our version is tossed in lemony vinaigrette, so it's refreshing and light. You can refrigerate the salad before serving so that the flavors really mesh, or even serve it warm.

2 pounds small red-skinned potatoes, unpeeled
½ cup olive oil
¼ cup fresh lemon juice
1 teaspoon lemon zest
Salt and pepper to taste
¼ cup fresh rosemary, finely chopped
¼ cup fresh thyme, finely chopped
3 scallions, thinly sliced

Cook potatoes in large pot of boiling salted water until tender, about 25 minutes. Drain and cool 15 minutes, then quarter. Whisk oil, lemon juice, and zest in small bowl to blend. Season with salt and pepper. Mix in rosemary, thyme, and scallions. Add potatoes to bowl with dressing and toss. Let stand 10 minutes. Refrigerate or serve immediately.

Parmesan Brussels Sprout

price $6 servings 4 price per servir

Someone needs to take these Brussels sprouts and serve them to every
claims to be offended by this mild and delicious vegetable. This method of
preparation masks the bitterness that so many dislike by coating them with a crispy
layer of savory cheese

1 pound Brussels sprouts, halved 1 teaspoon pepper
⅓ cup olive oil ½ cup Parmesan cheese, grated
2 teaspoons kosher salt

Preheat oven to 400°F. In large bowl, toss sprouts, olive oil, salt, and pepper. Bake 20
minutes in a baking dish, turning once, until sprouts begin to brown. Sprinkle Parmesan over
sprouts; return to oven additional 3–5 minutes, until cheese is melted and slightly browned.

Simple Roasted Asparagus

price $6 servings 4 price per serving $1.50

This delicious method for cooking asparagus is as simple and frugal as possible,
yet the resulting asparagus are classy and tasty. Season the asparagus liberally and
serve them plain, as a side dish, or over a salad.

1 bunch asparagus 2 teaspoons kosher salt
⅓ cup olive oil 1 teaspoon pepper

Preheat oven to 400°F. Snap thick ends off asparagus. In baking dish, toss asparagus,
olive oil, salt, and pepper. Bake 20 minutes, turning once, until asparagus are slightly
browned.

Spicy Sweet Potato Wedges

price $6   servings 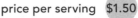 4   price per serving $1.50

*T*oo often, side dishes lack punch; they play the drab sidekick to the dazzling main course. If you're looking for a little role reversal, try a batch of these hot, flavorful potato wedges—a healthier alternate to French fries when you're craving a filling accompaniment to burgers, sandwiches, or anything else.

3 sweet potatoes, peeled and cut into 1" wedges
1 tablespoon olive oil
1 tablespoon brown sugar
1 teaspoon chili powder
¼ teaspoon cayenne pepper
1 teaspoon kosher salt

Preheat oven to 400°F. Toss potato wedges with olive oil, brown sugar, chili powder, cayenne pepper, and kosher salt. Bake on nonstick baking sheet 30 minutes, turning every 10 minutes, until browned.

Squash Soufflé

price $12   servings 6   price per serving $2

We imagine soufflés as requiring attentive care and precision. But for this dessert-like side, the entire preparation consists of blending a few ingredients together and baking them in the oven. Because it cooks in a large baking dish, there's no need to worry about it rising and falling. Instead, you can concentrate on enjoying the sweetness and spice that vanilla, cinnamon, and nutmeg infuse into this warm, nourishing dish.

1 (10-ounce) package frozen squash, defrosted
3 tablespoons butter
3 eggs
2 cups milk
½ cup flour
⅓ cup sugar
1 tablespoon vanilla extract
½ teaspoon nutmeg
½ teaspoon cinnamon

Preheat oven to 350°F. In small saucepan over low heat, stir together squash and butter until butter melts. In blender, combine eggs, milk, flour, sugar, and vanilla; blend until smooth. Add squash to blender; continue to mix until ingredients are blended well. Pour into greased 9" × 9" baking dish; sprinkle with nutmeg and cinnamon. Bake 1 hour and serve immediately.

Vegetarian Mexican Bean and Pepper Salad

price  $12   servings 6   price per serving $2

This is a vegetarian side dish that's full of protein. Serve it alongside fajitas or quesadillas so you can scoop this tangy salad on top.

2 (15-ounce) cans black beans, drained and rinsed
1 medium red bell pepper, diced
1 medium green bell pepper, diced
1 medium yellow bell pepper, diced
1 medium orange bell pepper, diced
1 cup fresh corn or 1 (15-ounce) can corn, drained
½ cup onion, diced
¼ cup fresh cilantro, chopped

DRESSING:
¼ cup olive oil
Juice of 2 limes
1 teaspoon cumin
⅛ teaspoon cayenne
1 tablespoon honey
Salt and pepper to taste

In large bowl, mix together beans, peppers, corn, onions, and cilantro. Separately, whisk together olive oil, lime juice, cumin, cayenne, honey, salt, and pepper. Toss bean mixture with dressing and serve.

Twice-Baked Parmesan Pot

price $10   servings 4   price per se

When we first started cooking, we scoffed at dishes puddings, appalled by their bold use of fatty ingredients and g... unattractive presentation. But we soon realized that our bias was unfounded, and we began to investigate ways to cut down the unhealthy aspects of some of these recipes. Here, twice-baked potatoes get a minor makeover with skim milk and minimal butter, but we're sure you'll still recognize the classic flavors.

4 large baking potatoes
2 scallions, thinly sliced
1 garlic clove
1 tablespoon butter, cut into small pieces
¼ cup skim milk
2 teaspoons salt
1 teaspoon pepper
¼ cup Parmesan cheese, plus extra for sprinkling
¼ teaspoon paprika

Preheat oven to 350°F. Using fork, pierce several holes in potatoes. Bake 45 minutes; remove from oven. Cut thin slice off top of each potato; scoop out soft inside, keeping skins intact. Sauté scallions and garlic until soft. In large bowl, mix potato insides with butter, milk, salt, pepper, garlic, scallions, and Parmesan; stir until well combined. Spoon mixture back into skins; dot tops with butter. Sprinkle with paprika and Parmesan. Return to oven; bake 15–20 minutes, until crispy.

Baked Beans with a Kick

price $6   servings 6   price per serving $1

The next time you break out baked beans, try this spicy, more flavorful version. Leave out the bacon and Worcestershire Sauce for a veggie version.

1 (15-ounce) can black beans with liquid
1 (28-ounce) can vegetarian baked beans with liquid
1 large onion, chopped
1 medium green bell pepper, chopped
¼ cup ketchup
2 tablespoons brown sugar, packed
2 tablespoons spicy mustard
2 tablespoons Worcestershire sauce
½ teaspoon garlic powder
3 strips bacon, cooked and chopped

Preheat oven to 350°F. Coat 9" × 13" baking dish with oil; pour in beans. Add all remaining ingredients; stir until well mixed. Cover with aluminum foil; bake 30 minutes. Remove foil; bake 1 hour, or until mixture is bubbly and onion and pepper are tender. Remove from oven and serve. Flavors improve when baked ahead and reheated.

MUFFiNS AND CUPCAKES

Banana-Chocolate Muffins

price $10   servings 12   price per serving $.85

When facing a pile of overly ripe bananas on your windowsill, it's exciting to have an option other than banana bread; these muffins make a delicious, quicker alternative. The unique speckled texture makes them particularly eye catching, and the chocolate adds a subtly sweet note that will have you craving them all day long.

½ cup rolled oats
1¼ cups skim milk
2 teaspoons vanilla extract
1½ cups flour
1 teaspoon baking powder
¼ teaspoon salt
½ cup brown sugar
1 cup dark chocolate, very finely chopped
1 egg, lightly beaten
½ cup butter, melted and cooled
1 very ripe banana, mashed

Preheat oven to 400°F. Line muffin tin with 12 paper liners. Combine oats, milk, and vanilla in bowl; let oats soak. In the meantime, in large bowl, combine flour, baking powder, salt, and sugar. Use fork to run through mixture and break up any clumps of sugar or flour. Stir in chocolate. To the oat mixture add eggs and butter. Add oat mixture and banana to large bowl; mix until just combined. Spoon batter into muffin tin; bake 18–20 minute. Transfer to cooling racks for several minutes and serve.

Big Apple Muffins

price $20   servings 18   price per serving $1.11

When we first learned that we'd both be moving to New York after graduating from college, we baked these muffins to celebrate. We even invested in an extra-large muffin pan for the occasion. These big apple muffins are almost like your typical apple muffins, but they're bigger and better and have walnuts and a streusel topping; an omen of good things to come. However, since big muffin pans are sometimes hard to find, this recipe is for regular-sized muffins.

2 cups all-purpose flour
½ teaspoon baking soda
1 teaspoon baking powder
1 teaspoon cinnamon
½ teaspoon salt
½ cup butter
½ cup granulated sugar
½ cup brown sugar
2 eggs
1¼ teaspoons vanilla
1½ cups Gala or McIntosh apple, shredded
½ cup apples Gala or McIntosh, chopped
¾ cup walnuts, chopped

STREUSEL TOPPING:

⅓ cup packed brown sugar
⅛ teaspoon ground cinnamon
1 tablespoon all-purpose flour
1 tablespoon butter

Preheat oven to 375°F. Line 18 regular-sized muffin cups with paper liners. Combine flour, baking soda, baking powder, cinnamon, and salt in medium bowl. In large bowl, beat together butter and sugar. Beat in eggs one at a time, then vanilla. Stir in apples and walnuts. Slowly stir in flour mixture until just combined. To make topping, mix ingredients with fingers until consistency resembles coarse meal. Spoon batter into muffin cups; sprinkle with topping. Cook 18 minutes for regular-sized muffins or 20–25 minutes for extra large. Transfer to cooling racks for several minutes and serve.

Chai Muffins with Figs and Oats

price $10 servings 12 price per serving $.85

*H*ealthy yet filling, these muffins are great for breakfast and brunch. Alanna used to tote one to class every morning, but after letting her classmates have a taste, she ended up having to bring enough for everyone sitting around her. Now, we "forget" to tell people when we've made them, and we keep them for ourselves.

1¼ cups soy milk
2 teabags chai tea
½ cup rolled oats
2 teaspoons vanilla extract
1½ cups whole-wheat flour
¾ cup light brown sugar
1 teaspoon salt
3 teaspoons baking powder
½ cup chopped dried figs
1 egg, lightly beaten
6 tablespoons canola oil

Preheat oven to 375°F. Line 12 muffin cups with paper liners. Heat milk in saucepan until hot to touch. Remove from heat; add tea bags and let steep 1 minute, until milk is light caramel brown. Put oats in small bowl; pour milk and vanilla over, stir briefly, and let sit. In medium bowl, combine flour, sugar, salt, and baking powder. Stir in figs, then egg and oil to lightly coat. Pour oat mixture over top; stir until just combined. Pour batter into muffin cups; top with few extra oats. Bake 20 minutes. Transfer to cooling racks for several minutes and serve.

Chocolate Cupcakes with Mint Icing

price $25   servings 24   price per serving $1

*T*hese are the perfect cupcakes for anyone who adores peppermint patties, peppermint mochas, and other mint-chocolate combinations. The cupcakes are chocolate, and we top them with a sweet but understated peppermint icing. Garnishing the treats with a small mint leaf is a small but crucial touch that keeps these cupcakes festive around the holidays and brightly fresh year-round.

1½ cups all-purpose flour
¾ cup cocoa powder
¼ teaspoon baking soda
2 teaspoons baking powder
¼ teaspoon salt
¼ cup butter, softened
1 cup sugar
½ cup brown sugar
2 eggs, room temperature
1 teaspoon vanilla extract
1 cup warm milk

FROSTING:
1 cup butter
4–5 cups powdered sugar
¼ cup milk
⅛ teaspoon peppermint extract
¼ cup small fresh mint leaves, for garnish

Preheat oven to 350°F. Line 24 muffin cups with paper liners. In medium bowl, combine flour, cocoa powder, baking soda, baking powder, and salt. In large bowl, cream together butter and sugars. Beat in eggs one at a time; stir in vanilla. Alternate adding small amounts of flour and milk to sugar mixture; combine well. Pour batter into cups; bake 15–17 minutes, until knife comes out clean. To make frosting, beat butter with electric mixer until creamy. Add 4 cups powdered sugar, milk, and extract; beat until combined. Add more sugar to thicken frosting if needed. Frost cupcakes, top with mint leaf, and serve.

Double Chocolate Chip Peanut Butter Muffins

price $16   servings 12   price per serving $1.30

*F*or this muffin recipe, we included healthier versions of ingredients whenever possible, convincing ourselves that using reduced-fat peanut butter and skim milk justified adding extra chocolate chips. Fortunately, our sneaky substitutions are not noticeable, and these boast a strong chocolate flavor that isn't overwhelmingly sweet.

2¼ cups whole-wheat flour

½ cup granulated sugar

¾ cup brown sugar

2 tablespoons unsweetened cocoa powder

1 teaspoon salt

2 teaspoons baking soda

2 eggs, lightly beaten

1 cup skim milk

6 tablespoons butter substitute or butter, melted

½ cup reduced-fat peanut butter

¾ cup white chocolate chips

¾ cup chocolate chips

Extra flour to coat chocolate chips

Preheat oven to 400°F. Line 12 muffin cups with paper liners. In large bowl, mix together flour, sugars, cocoa powder, salt, and baking soda. In separate bowl, mix eggs, milk, butter, and peanut butter. Add wet ingredients to dry ingredients; stir until just combined. Coat chocolate chips in extra flour so they don't sink to bottom of muffins; mix into batter. Fill muffin liners almost full with batter; bake 20 minutes. Transfer to cooling racks for several minutes and serve.

"Jacqui" Muffins

price $18   servings 12   price per serving $1.50

These muffins were inspired by Alanna's college roommate. They have almost every ingredient we could imagine adding to muffins—nuts, seeds, oats, raisins, and orange zest. The result is an intensely healthy, moist, and scrumptious muffin that is perfect any time.

1 cup all-purpose flour
1 cup whole-wheat flour
1¼ cups granulated sugar
¾ teaspoon baking soda
1½ teaspoons baking powder
½ teaspoon salt
1½ teaspoons cinnamon
2 teaspoons orange zest
½ cup walnuts, toasted and coarsely shopped
1 cup coconut
½ cup rolled oats
⅓ cup golden raisins
⅓ cup pumpkin seeds
4 eggs
1½ teaspoons vanilla extract
1 cup canola oil
2 cups raw carrot, grated
1 large apple, peeled and grated (try Gala)

Preheat oven to 350°F. Line 12 muffin cups with paper liners. In large bowl, combine flours, sugar, baking soda, baking powder, salt, and cinnamon. Stir in orange zest, walnuts, coconut, rolled oats, raisins, and pumpkin seeds. In separate bowl, lightly beat eggs; whisk in vanilla and oil. Add wet ingredients to dry ingredients; stir until just combined. Add carrot and apple; mix well. Spoon batter into muffin cups; bake 20 minutes. Transfer to cooling racks for several minutes and serve.

Luckiest Muffins

price $12   servings 12   price per serving $1

These fun-loving, bright muffins are great for kids and holidays, especially around St. Patrick's Day. The marshmallows melt into the batter, so you end up with rainbow-streaked muffins that are as festive as they are delicious.

2 cups self-rising flour
1 teaspoon baking powder
¼ cup butter
⅓ cup superfine sugar
2 eggs, lightly beaten
1 cup milk
1 teaspoon vanilla extract
1½ cups marshmallows from Lucky Charms

Preheat oven to 400°F. Line 12 muffin cups with paper liners. Mix flour and baking powder together in large bowl; add butter and rub into mixture. Stir in sugar. In separate bowl, combine eggs, milk, and vanilla; stir into flour mix. Fold in charms until combined; spoon batter into muffin cups. Bake 20 minutes, until well risen and golden. Transfer to cooling racks for several minutes and serve.

Orange Creamsicle Cupcakes

price $12   servings 18   price per serving $.70

*T*hese cupcakes are inspired by one of our favorite cold treats: Creamsicles. Alanna has always been a big fan of the orange-cream combination—she even used to put vanilla ice cream in her orange juice when she was little. These cupcakes are a classier way to capture the essence of the Creamsicle, with a pure vanilla cake and a creamy orange frosting.

1½ cups self-rising flour

1¼ cups all-purpose flour

1 cup (2 sticks) unsalted butter, softened

2 cups sugar

4 large eggs, room temperature

1 cup milk

1 teaspoon vanilla extract

FROSTING:

½ cup (1 stick) unsalted butter, softened

6–8 cups confectioners' sugar

¼ cup orange juice, fresh squeezed

1 teaspoon orange zest, grated

1 teaspoon vanilla extract

1 drop red and yellow food coloring (optional)

Preheat oven to 350°F. Line 18 muffin cups with paper liners. In small bowl, combine flours; set aside. In large bowl, cream butter until smooth. Add sugar gradually; beat until fluffy, about 3 minutes. Add eggs 1 at a time, beating well after each. Incorporate dry ingredients in 3 batches, alternating with milk and vanilla. Spoon batter into cupcake papers ¾ full. Bake 20–25 minutes, or until tester inserted in center comes out clean. Transfer to cooling racks for several minutes before frosting.

For frosting, cream butter with hand mixer in medium bowl. Gradually add 4 cups sugar, 1 cup at a time, beating well after each (about 2 minutes). Add orange juice, zest, and vanilla. Add remaining sugar until frosting reaches your desired thickness. If desired, add food coloring and mix thoroughly. Frosting can be stored in airtight container at room temperature up to 3 days.

PB&J (Hold the Crust) Muffins

price $12   servings 12   price per serving $1

*T*hese muffins are a beautiful adaptation of the classic whole-wheat peanut butter and jelly sandwich. They are moist, soft, and very much a muffin—not too sweet, but so good. We enjoy the warm, wheat taste, and the consistency is perfect despite the fact we don't use butter and choose reduced-fat peanut butter. These are simple and delicious, much like the sandwich that inspires them.

2¼ cups whole-wheat flour
2 teaspoons baking powder
½ teaspoon salt
⅔ cup brown sugar
6 tablespoons butter substitute, melted and cooled
½ cup reduced-fat crunchy peanut butter
2 eggs
1 cup skim milk
⅓ cup jam or jelly

Preheat oven to 375°F. Line 12 muffin cups with paper liners. In large bowl, combine flour, baking powder, salt, and brown sugar. In medium bowl, combine butter substitute, peanut butter, eggs, and milk; whisk together until smooth. Pour wet ingredients into dry mixture; stir into batter. Fill each tin halfway with batter, add heaping teaspoon of jelly, and fill to top with more batter. Bake 17 minutes, or until knife comes out clean. Transfer to cooling racks for several minutes and serve warm.

COOKiES
AND BARS

Chocolate-Covered Toasted Rice Treats

price $12   servings 12   price per serving $1

We know these are special because Alex's Colombian grandmother, who makes the best homemade arepas and empanadas ever, reported that these treats were the most delicious things she has tasted in her entire life. They are simple and fun and go well with any topping imaginable.

3 tablespoons butter
1 bag marshmallows
1 box toasted rice cereal
2 cups semisweet chocolate chips
1 cup mini M&Ms
1 cup Heath bits
1 cup sweetened coconut

Melt butter in large pot. Add marshmallows; stir until melted. Add cereal; stir. Spread into 9" × 12" baking dish; allow to cool. Once cool, cut into small rectangles. In microwave-safe bowl, melt chocolate chips in 30-second increments, stirring after each, until fully melted (or melt slowly in a double boiler so chocolate doesn't burn). Dip treats into melted chocolate; place on parchment paper. While chocolate is still warm, sprinkle with M&Ms, Heath bits, or coconut. Allow chocolate to harden in cool place; serve.

Chocolate-Dipped S'mores

price $6   servings 8   price per serving $.75

We foster a true love of s'mores. It's not a seasonal love where we'll make a few sandwiches per summer, but rather a love *so* real that in the winter we resort to making them in the microwave or toasting marshmallows on chopsticks over a gas stove (not an activity we recommend). These updated s'mores are a perfect frugal dessert for guests who are young at heart.

1 cup marshmallow fluff
8 graham crackers
1 cup chocolate chips
1 tablespoon cream

Spread fluff on a graham cracker; top with another graham cracker. Mix chocolate and cream in microwavable bowl; melt in microwave (heat about 2 minutes, stopping every 30 seconds to stir, or melt gradually over a double boiler). Dip graham cracker and fluff in melted chocolate; let cool on wax paper. Serve when chocolate is hardened.

Chocolate-Marshmallow Brownies

price $12   servings 12   price per serving $1

We've tried many from-scratch brownie recipes that are too cakey or too dense or too sweet or too gooey; this one is just right. The consistency of the brownie is perfect, and the marshmallow and fudge layers are truly the icing on the cake. We advise making the brownies the day before you plan to frost them so they have enough time to cool.

½ cup butter
2 ounces unsweetened chocolate
1 cup sugar
2 large eggs
¾ cup flour
¼ teaspoon salt
½ teaspoon baking powder
½ teaspoon vanilla
30 marshmallows, cut in half

FUDGE FROSTING:
3 ounces unsweetened chocolate
3 tablespoons butter
½ teaspoon vanilla
2 tablespoons milk
2 cups confectioners' sugar

Preheat oven to 350°F. In small saucepan over medium-low heat, melt butter and chocolate. Stir in sugar until just dissolved; immediately remove from heat. Pour into medium mixing bowl; beat in eggs 1 at a time until mixture is glossy. Add dry ingredients and vanilla. Bake 15–18 minutes in greased 9" × 9" × 2" square pan. Remove from oven; cover with marshmallows. Return to oven 5 minutes. Cool completely, several hours or overnight. For frosting, melt chocolate and butter in small saucepan. Pour into mixing bowl; add vanilla, milk, and sugar. Beat until smooth. Spread over brownies, allow fudge to harden, and serve.

Chocolate Meringues

price $8   servings 6   price per serving $1.35

When you're making flan, save the egg whites for these simple meringues.

4 egg whites, room temperature   1 cup powdered sugar
⅛ teaspoon salt   ½ teaspoon vanilla extract
⅛ teaspoon cream of tartar   1 tablespoon cocoa powder

Preheat oven to 200°F. In large bowl, use electric mixer to beat egg whites, salt, and cream of tartar. When whites form stiff peaks, gradually add ½ cup sugar. As peaks become glossy, fold in remaining sugar, vanilla extract, and cocoa powder. Line 2 cookie sheets with parchment or wax paper. Use pastry bag or spoon to form 1" mounds of mixture on cookie sheets. Bake until meringues are firm and lightly browned, 1½–2 hours. Transfer to cooling racks for several minutes and serve. Makes 2 dozen cookies.

Stir-Me-Not Bars

price $12   servings 12   price per serving $1

These bars are irresistibly tasty and require almost no effort!

1 stick butter, melted   12 ounces chocolate chips
1½ cups graham cracker crumbs   1 (14-ounce) can sweetened condensed milk
1 cup sweetened flaked coconut   1 cup chopped walnuts

Preheat oven to 350°F. Pour batter into 9" × 13" pan and top with crumbs, coconut, chocolate chips, milk, and walnuts. Do not stir. Bake 35–40 minutes. Let cool before cutting into bars. Makes 2 dozen bars.

Danny's Sweet and Salty Almond Cookies

price $12   servings 12   price per serving $1

*T*hese cookies are predominantly sweet, with a slight savory, salty note. They're funkier than your average cookie and are a huge hit with fans of other sweet-and-salty dessert foods like chocolate-covered pretzels or potato chips.

1½ cups all-purpose flour
½ teaspoon kosher salt or sea salt
½ teaspoon baking soda
1½ teaspoons cinnamon
½ cup butter (1 stick), room temperature
½ cup granulated sugar
½ cup brown sugar
1 large egg
1 teaspoon vanilla extract
2 cups roasted salted almonds, coarsely chopped

Preheat oven to 350°F. In small bowl, combine flour, salt, baking soda, and cinnamon. In separate, larger bowl, cream together butter and sugars; beat in egg and vanilla. Gradually beat in dry ingredients; stir in almonds. Form into cookie rounds; place on greased baking sheets. Bake 12 minutes, until they begin to show a golden color around edges. Transfer to cooling racks for several minutes and serve. Makes about 2 dozen cookies.

Grandma's Italian Cookies

price $15   servings 10–15   price per serving $1

*T*his is a recipe for traditional Italian cookies that we first discovered through a close friend's grandmother. Because they're often made for big parties, each batch produces a lot of cookies. We once multiplied the recipe and made more than 100 but still managed to finish these light and buttery treats within a week.

½ cup (1 stick) butter, melted
2 cups sugar
3 eggs
4 cups flour
1 teaspoon baking soda
1 teaspoon salt
16 ounces fat-free ricotta cheese
2 teaspoons vanilla extract

ICING:
¼ pound margarine
3⅓ cups powdered sugar
1 teaspoon vanilla extract
1 teaspoon skim milk
Colored sprinkles (optional)

Preheat oven to 350°F. Cream butter and sugar in small bowl; add eggs 1 at a time. In large bowl, sift together flour, baking soda, and salt. Mix liquid mixture into dry ingredients. Add ricotta and vanilla; mix. Spoon dough onto baking sheets, making each cookie the size of a quarter and placing at least 1"–2" apart. Bake 12 minutes, or until brown on the bottom (they will still be fairly white on top). Transfer to cooling racks for several minutes before frosting.

To make icing, add margarine to powdered sugar; mix. Mix in vanilla and milk. When cool, ice and top with sprinkles. Makes 4 dozen cookies.

Lemon–Poppy Seed Cookies

price $12   servings 12   price per serving $1

As we mention frequently, we don't believe in the phrase "too much lemon." These cookies are the culinary embodiment of that idea. They're very, very lemony, which is precisely why we bake them.

Juice of 1 lemon
1 stick butter
⅔ cup sugar
1 egg
2 teaspoons vanilla
Zest of 1 lemon
1½ cups flour
½ teaspoon baking powder
½ teaspoon salt
1 tablespoon poppy seeds

Preheat oven to 350°F. In small saucepan, bring lemon juice to boil; reduce by half. Melt ½ stick of butter into lemon juice; set aside to cool. Cream together remaining ½ stick of butter and sugar; add egg and vanilla. In separate small bowl, combine lemon zest, flour, baking powder, and salt. Mix lemon juice and butter into wet ingredients; gradually add dry ingredients. Mix in poppy seeds. Scoop 1" dough balls onto greased cookie sheet; bake 10–12 minutes. Transfer to cooling racks for several minutes and serve. Makes 1 dozen cookies.

Hershey Kiss Peanut Blossoms

price $12   servings 12   price per serving $1

You may recognize these from eating them during the holidays, from the grocery store box, or maybe from your own recipe. We included our favorite version of them because despite their ubiquity, we still think they're special.

1¾ cups flour
½ cup sugar, plus additional for rolling
1 teaspoon baking soda
½ teaspoon salt
½ cup butter (1 stick), room temperature
½ cup brown sugar, packed
½ cup peanut butter
2 tablespoons milk
1 teaspoon vanilla extract
1 egg
48 milk chocolate Kisses, unwrapped

Preheat oven to 375°F. In medium bowl, combine flour, white sugar, baking soda, and salt. In large bowl, combine butter, brown sugar, peanut butter, milk, vanilla, and egg; beat well with electric mixer. Add dry ingredients; mix thoroughly with wooden spoon until stiff dough forms. Place additional sugar in shallow bowl or plate. Roll dough into 1" balls; roll in sugar and place 2" apart on cookie sheet. Flatten lightly with fingers; bake 10–12 minutes, or until golden brown. Remove from oven; immediately press 1 Kiss firmly into each cookie. Remove from cookie sheets; let cool on wire rack. Makes 4 dozen cookies.

Pistachio Biscotti

price $12   servings 8   price per serving $1.50

*T*hese biscotti aren't particularly sweet, but they have a wonderful texture and a subtle nutty flavor that makes them perfect for dipping in coffee any time of day.

1½ cups shelled raw unsalted natural pistachios
2¼ cups unbleached all-purpose flour
1 teaspoon baking powder
¼ teaspoon salt
3 eggs, room temperature
1 cup sugar
1 teaspoon vanilla extract
¼ teaspoon lemon zest

Preheat oven to 350°F. Toast pistachios in oven 5 minutes; cool and coarsely chop. In medium bowl, combine flour, baking powder, and salt. In large bowl, beat together eggs, sugar, and vanilla with electric mixer until mixture forms ribbons. Gently stir in flour mixture until just incorporated; fold in pistachios and lemon zest. On greased or parchment-lined baking sheet, form dough into 2 smooth, 3" wide loaves; bake 25 minutes. Cool 10 minutes; cut into ½" thick slices. Lower oven temperature to 300°F . Bake for an additional 10–12 minutes on each side until just brown. Serve with coffee or tea.

CAKES AND PiES

Blueberry Coffee Cake

price $10   servings 10   price per serving $1

*B*lueberries are among our favorite fruits, so we can't imagine going a whole winter without cooking with them. This coffee cake satiates our blueberry cravings, and because it tastes just as yummy with frozen blueberries as with fresh ones, we can bake it year-round. For a healthier version, just skip the crumb topping.

¼ cup butter, softened, plus 1 tablespoon for greasing pan

8 ounces nonfat cream cheese

1 cup sugar

1 egg

1 cup all-purpose flour

1 teaspoon baking powder

¼ teaspoon salt

1 teaspoon cinnamon

1 teaspoon lemon zest

1 teaspoon vanilla extract

2 cups frozen blueberries

CRUMB TOPPING:

2 tablespoons cold butter, cut into small pieces

¼ cup all-purpose flour

½ cup dark brown sugar

1 teaspoon ground cinnamon

Preheat oven to 350°F. Cream together butter and cream cheese using electric mixer on medium speed. Beat in sugar and egg. Combine flour, baking powder, salt, cinnamon, and lemon zest; add to butter mixture. Mix in vanilla; fold in berries. Pour batter into greased 9" round cake pan. For crumb topping, combine all ingredients in small bowl; mix together with fork until crumbly. Sprinkle over batter; bake 1 hour. Let cool before serving.

Caramel Apple Tartlets

price $8   servings   12   price per serving $.70

These tartlets draw inspiration from extreme caramel apples—you know, the ones with caramel, chocolate, nuts, the works. The tartlets taste just as delicious and stick to your teeth with the same persistence (in case you were worried about that). They make a great dessert for a crowd.

1 recipe pie crust (see page 186)
20 wrapped individual caramel candies
2 tart apples, peeled and sliced into 1" pieces
½ cup walnuts, toasted and chopped
½ cup chocolate chips

Preheat oven to 350°F. Roll out dough; cut into 3" rounds. Place rounds in mini tartlet pans; weight down by covering with foil and filling with pie weights or rice. Bake 15 minutes with weights; remove weights and foil and bake additional 5 minutes. Melt caramels in microwave by heating 30 seconds, then stirring until melted. Add 1 teaspoon caramel to bottom of each tart; fill with apple. Top apples with toasted walnuts; drizzle with additional caramel. Melt chocolate chips by microwaving 30 seconds then stirring until melted; drizzle on top. You can melt caramels or chocolate gently in a double boiler as an alternative to the microwave. Allow chocolate to harden and serve.

Cheesecake with Berry Sauce

price $20   servings 10   price per serving $2

*S*urprisingly, cheesecake is among the simplest desserts to make, and it's such a crowd pleaser that it would be worth far more effort than it takes. Use frozen berries for the sauce in the winter or any seasonal berries you may find.

CRUST:

2 cups graham cracker crumbs

3 tablespoons sugar

1 stick butter, melted

CHEESECAKE FILLING:

3 (8-ounce) packages cream cheese, softened

1 cup sugar

3 eggs

¼ cup half-and-half

¾ cup low-fat buttermilk

1½ tablespoons lemon juice

1 teaspoon vanilla extract

BERRY SAUCE:

2 cups fresh or frozen mixed berries

⅓ cup plus 1 tablespoon sugar

1 tablespoon brandy

1½ teaspoons lemon juice

1 teaspoon cornstarch

Berries for garnish (optional)

Preheat oven to 350°F. To make crust, mix together crumbs and sugar. Melt butter; stir into crumb mixture until well combined. Press into bottom of greased springform pan; set aside. With hand mixer, combine cream cheese and sugar until fluffy. Add eggs one at a time, then gradually mix in half-and-half and buttermilk; add lemon juice and vanilla. Pour over crust. Place springform pan in large baking dish filled with water. Bake 50–60 minutes, or until golden brown and firm. Let cool to room temperature before removing from pan. To make berry topping, combine berries, sugar, brandy, and lemon juice in medium saucepan. Simmer until berries begin to break down, about 10 minutes. Strain through sieve into bowl, pressing to extract as much juice as possible. Return strained juice to saucepan; bring back to simmer. Add cornstarch; continue to simmer until sauce begins to thicken, about 5 minutes. Let cool; serve over cheesecake with fresh berries.

Hot Fudge Pudding Cake

price $12   servings 6   price per serving $2

*T*his cake tastes like warm brownie batter that you can scoop over ice cream for the tastiest chocolate delight imaginable.

1 cup flour
¾ cup sugar
2 tablespoons plus ¼ cup cocoa powder
2 tablespoons baking powder
¼ teaspoon salt
½ cup milk
2 tablespoons melted butter
1 cup brown sugar
1¾ cups hot water

Preheat oven to 350°F. Combine flour, sugar, 2 tablespoons cocoa powder, baking powder, salt, milk, and melted butter in large bowl; mix well. Spread into ungreased 8" × 6" brownie pan. In small bowl, mix brown sugar and ¼ cup cocoa powder; sprinkle evenly over batter. Gently pour hot water over entire mixture. Set brownie pan on cookie sheet; bake 45 minutes. Transfer to cooling rack for several minutes; serve warm with ice cream.

Moist Apple Cake with Sherry Glaze

price $20   servings 8   price per serving $2.50

*T*his cake is heart-meltingly moist and thick, as it's packed with chopped apples, nuts, and spices. The sherry glaze crystallizes beautifully over the cake and adds a complementary kick to each bite. This also happens to be our favorite cake batter, and we think the opportunity to lick the bowl is itself a reason to bake this cake.

3 cups all-purpose flour

1½ teaspoons baking soda

½ teaspoon salt

1 teaspoon cinnamon

⅛ teaspoon nutmeg

1 cup butter

2 cups sugar

2 teaspoons vanilla

3 eggs

1 cup sour cream

2 cups walnuts, chopped

3 cups Gala apples, peeled, cored, and chopped

SHERRY GLAZE:

½ cup sherry

1½ cups sugar

Preheat oven to 350°F. In small bowl, combine flour, baking soda, salt, cinnamon, and nutmeg. In large bowl, use mixer to cream together butter and sugar until thick. Add vanilla; beat in eggs 1 at a time. Alternate beating dry ingredients and sour cream into butter mixture. Stir in nuts and apples. Pour batter into greased tube or Bundt pan. Bake 90 minutes; remove from pan and transfer to cooling rack. To make glaze, combine sherry and sugar in small pan over medium heat. Bring to a boil; boil 8 minutes, then let cool 10 minutes, until it begins to become opaque. Pour glaze over cake; let drip down sides. Serve once glaze has cooled.

Peanut Butter Ice Cream Cake

price **$18**   servings **6**   price per serving **$3**

*I*ce cream cakes are a tradition for birthdays in Alanna's family, and this one is ideal for peanut butter lovers. Half of the cake is frozen whipped cream and the other half is peanut butter icing, so each bite contains a delicious duo of sweet and light cream with thick peanut butter. The chopped peanuts and chocolate wafer crust lend texture and crunch.

3 pints peanut butter ice cream

1 box chocolate wafer cookies

2 tablespoons unsalted butter, melted

1½ cups well-chilled heavy cream

1 teaspoon vanilla

¾ cup peanuts, chopped

Begin preparing cake 1 day ahead. Set out ice cream 15 minutes to soften. Grind wafers in food processor until they resemble coarse meal. Set aside ¾ cup cookie crumbs; add melted butter to remaining crumbs to form crumbly crust. Press crust into bottom and 1" up sides of a 9" springform pan. Freeze crust 30 minutes. After crust has been freezing for 30 minutes, remove ice cream from freezer to soften for 15 minutes. Spread softened ice cream evenly over crust. Return to freezer for 30 minutes. Use electric mixer to whip heavy cream with vanilla until soft peaks form. Gently fold reserved cookie crumbs and chopped peanuts into whipped cream. Spread over cake; cover with foil and return to freezer for at least 4 hours, or overnight. Before releasing cake from pan, wrap warm, dampened kitchen towel around outside of pan to loosen cake. Remove cake, transfer to large plate, and serve immediately.

Pie Crust

price $8 servings 8 price per serving $1

*H*ere's a pie crust recipe that turns out exactly how we like it—flaky yet soft.

1¼ cups all-purpose flour
2 teaspoons granulated sugar
½ teaspoon salt

7 tablespoons cold butter, cut into ½" pieces
3 tablespoons cold water

Combine dry ingredients. Use hands, fork, or food processor to rub dry ingredients into butter until coarse meal forms. Drizzle with cold water; stir until dough comes together. Wrap in plastic wrap and flatten into a disk. Refrigerate at least 1 hour before rolling out.

Pumpkin Bread

price $8 servings 8 price per serving $1

*W*e love the amazing smell of warm and spicy pumpkin bread as it begins wafting from the oven. Here, the combination of spices is balanced, not overwhelming.

3½ cups flour
1 teaspoon baking powder
2 teaspoons baking soda
½ teaspoon ground cloves
2 teaspoons salt

1 teaspoon cinnamon
1 teaspoon ground nutmeg
1 teaspoon ground allspice
3 cups sugar

1 cup vegetable oil
4 eggs, beaten
12-ounce can pumpkin
⅔ cup water

Preheat oven to 350°F. In medium bowl, combine flour, baking powder, baking soda, cloves, salt, cinnamon, nutmeg, and allspice. In separate bowl, combine sugar, oil, and eggs; add pumpkin. Gradually add dry ingredients to wet ingredients. Add water; stir until combined. Pour into 2 greased loaf pans; bake 1 hour.

Festive Angel Food Cake

price $12　　servings 8　　price per serving $1.50

As huge angel food cake fans, we were thrilled to discover that we could add sprinkles to the batter. They look great and don't discolor the entire cake as we feared they might. This cake is fluffy and soft, and it's surprisingly easy to eat through half of it before you even realize it.

1½ cups powdered sugar
1 cup flour
¼ teaspoon salt
12 egg whites, room temperature
1½ teaspoons cream of tartar
1 cup granulated sugar
1 teaspoon vanilla extract
½ cup rainbow sprinkles

Preheat oven to 350°F; set oven rack in lower ⅓ of oven. Sift powdered sugar, flour, and salt together; set aside. Beat egg whites with mixer until frothy. Add cream of tartar; beat at medium speed until whites form soft peaks. Gradually beat in granulated sugar until thoroughly combined; beat in vanilla. Gradually sprinkle sifted flour mixture into batter; fold in with spatula. Fold in sprinkles. Pour batter into angel food cake pan. Bake 40 minutes, until top is lightly golden. Invert pan; cool completely. To remove, run knife around outer edge of pan and shake gently. Serve with Cool Whip, fresh fruit, or chocolate sauce.

Tartlets with Blackberries and Lime

price $15   servings 6   price per serving $2.50

*T*he best word to describe these mini tartlets is "lovely," followed closely by "petite" and "adorable." They'll make you pucker your lips, smile sweetly, and lick them, then reach for more.

DOUGH:
1¼ cups all-purpose flour
2 teaspoons granulated sugar
¼ teaspoon salt
7 tablespoons cold butter
3 tablespoons cold water

LIME FILLING:
3 large eggs
¾ cup granulated sugar
½ cup fresh lime juice
6 tablespoons unsalted butter,
    cut into ½" cubes
1 teaspoon finely grated fresh lime
    zest

GLAZED BLACKBERRIES:
¼ cup powdered sugar
¼ cup water
1 tablespoon fresh lime juice
2 cups fresh blackberries

For dough, combine dry ingredients; rub into butter until mixture resembles coarse meal. Drizzle with cold water; stir until dough comes together. Refrigerate at least 1 hour. For filling, whisk together eggs, sugar, and lime juice; add butter. Pour into a small saucepan and cook over moderately low heat, whisking constantly, until bubbles appear on surface, 8–10 minutes. Immediately pour through sieve into bowl, discarding solids. Cool to room temperature, stirring occasionally. Stir in zest; chill, covered, at least 1 hour. For glazed berries, boil powdered sugar, water, and lime juice in small saucepan over moderate heat 2 minutes, stirring. Toss berries into glaze; let cool. Preheat oven to 350°F. Press dough into mini tart pans; bake 10 minutes with pie weights or substitute (try tin foil filled with dry rice or beans), then additional 5 minutes without, until tarts become light brown. Let shells cool; fill with lime filling and top with berries.

MORE DESSERTS

Bananas Flambé

price $10   servings 4   price per serving $2.50

This is one of Alex's signature recipes. It's also one of the simplest and most impressive dishes to make for an audience. Alex made this on our first date, and it was an unbelievable culinary performance. Neither of us are huge banana people, but we continue to love this dish every time we make it, especially when we get to scrape crispy, caramelized banana pieces from the bottom of the pan.

2 tablespoons butter
3 tablespoons dark brown sugar
3 bananas, sliced
1 ounce dark rum or brandy
Vanilla ice cream (optional)

Heat butter in pan; melt sugar. Add bananas; cook until soft, about 3 minutes. Move bananas to half of pan; move that side of pan off of heat (so heat is beneath empty half of pan). Add rum or brandy to banana half of pan; quickly tilt pan so rum or brandy and bananas flow to hot and empty side of pan, allowing alcohol to touch flame. At this point, the alcohol should catch fire; shake pan to cook bananas in flames. Flames should die down after a few seconds. Remove bananas from heat; serve over ice cream.

Candied Pecans

price $10   servings 10   price per serving $1

*T*his dessert is dangerously addictive, as the pecans are lightly coated in a citrus sugar that brings out their delicious nutty flavor. We recommend gathering a group if you are going to make them, otherwise you may end up accidentally guilty of downing an entire batch in one sitting.

1 cup sugar
¼ teaspoon salt
½ teaspoon cinnamon
1 egg white
1 tablespoon orange juice
1 pound pecan halves (3–4 cups)

Preheat oven to 350°F. In small bowl, combine sugar, salt, and cinnamon. In separate large bowl, beat egg white and orange juice until frothy. Add pecan halves to egg mixture; coat well. Add sugar mixture to large bowl; toss to coat. Place on large baking pan covered with tin foil, spreading evenly. Bake 25–30 minutes, stirring every 8–10 minutes. Remove from pan immediately; cool before serving.

Fruity Cookie Pizza

price $20   servings 10   price per serving $2

This is a spectacular party dessert. The sugar-cookie base absorbs some of the flavor from toppings, yet each bite is uniquely delicious because of the different varieties of fruit. The cookie is moist with a great vanilla flavor, and the cream cheese sauce is just sweet enough to complement the fruit without overpowering it. Whenever we serve this, everyone goes back for seconds and cleans their plates.

½ cup butter, softened
¾ cup granulated sugar
1 egg
1¼ cups all-purpose flour
1 teaspoon cream of tartar
½ teaspoon baking soda
¼ teaspoon salt

TOPPING:
1 (8-ounce) package cream cheese
½ cup white sugar
2 teaspoons vanilla extract
16 ounces strawberries, sliced thinly
1 kiwi, peeled and sliced thinly
8 ounces blackberries, halved
1 mango, peeled and sliced thinly

In large bowl, cream together butter and sugar until smooth; mix in egg. In separate bowl, combine flour, cream of tartar, baking soda, and salt; beat into butter mixture until just blended. Chill at least 1 hour. Preheat oven to 350°F. Roll dough into a circle ¼"–½" thick; place on large nonstick or greased cookie sheet. Bake 10 minutes, until edges are golden brown. Cool completely; transfer carefully to serving plate (it's okay if it breaks a little, the topping will hold it together) In large bowl, beat cream cheese with sugar and vanilla until light. Spread on cooled crust; arrange fruit on top. Chill, slice, and serve.

Cherry Bread Pudding

price $12   servings 4   price per serving $3

This version of bread pudding includes less cream, butter, and fatty milk than you'll find in almost any other dessert recipe, but we assure you that taste has not been compromised. The lightness of the pudding makes it especially fitting for summertime, and any fruit in season will work beautifully. This recipe makes individual dishes, so we don't have to fight over who gets to eat more.

2 tablespoons butter or butter substitute
8 pieces cinnamon raisin bread, cut into 1" squares
2 teaspoons cinnamon
4 tablespoons sugar
2 cups skim milk
4 eggs
1 cup cherries, pits removed and coarsely chopped
⅔ cup dried cranberries
Powdered sugar

Preheat oven to 350°F. In medium bowl, melt butter; add bread, cinnamon, and sugar and toss until bread is coated. In separate bowl, whisk together milk and eggs. Pour over bread; allow to sit, covered and refrigerated, at least 15 minutes, then add cherries and dried cranberries. Fill 4 ramekins ¾ full with bread mixture. Bake 30 minutes, until tops have begun to brown. Dust with powdered sugar before serving.

Vanilla Ice Cream and Strawberry Brownie Bombs

price $12 servings 6 price per serving $2

These little ice cream treats have nothing to do with bombs, but they are an inventive way to serve individual ice cream desserts that are both beautiful and simple. Feel free to substitute other fruit for the strawberries, as long as you slice it thinly and make sure it's small enough to fit within the muffin tin.

1 cup strawberries, thinly sliced

1 pint vanilla ice cream, softened

1 cup crumbled brownies (we recommend Trader Joe's Brownie Bites Cookies or any other store-bought brownies)

Chocolate sauce (to serve)

Line 6 muffin cups with plastic wrap. Line each cup with sliced strawberries; fill with softened ice cream. Push crumbled brownies on top of ice cream. Put muffin tin in freezer at least 2 hours. Remove from tin by pulling out plastic wrap. Serve brownie-side down with chocolate sauce drizzled on top.

Minted Fruit Salad

price $12   servings 4   price per serving $3

This fruit-mint-sugar combination can transform any fruit salad into an exquisite dessert. Peaches and strawberries aren't the only combination, but do this while peaches are still in season and you'll hardly need the sugar.

12 ounces strawberries, hulled and halved
3 peaches, pitted and cut into 1" pieces
2 tablespoons sugar
2 tablespoons mint, finely chopped
⅛ teaspoon vanilla
Whipped cream (optional)

Combine fruit, sugar, mint, and vanilla in medium bowl; toss to coat. Serve chilled with whipped cream.

Dessert Kebabs

price $30   servings 15   price per serving $2

These kebabs look extravagant, but they're fun if you enjoy magic wands and mini-dessert samples. We loved using different fruit and chocolate desserts, but you can make your wands out of any little desserts you choose.

15 Chocolate-Covered Toasted Rice Treats (see page 170)
15 chocolate-covered strawberries
15 chocolate mini muffins (store bought or homemade)
3 star fruits, each cut into 5 slices (or any other decorative fruit, such as pineapple)
15 wooden skewers

Skewer a rice treat and push to bottom of skewer. Next, skewer a strawberry, then a muffin, and top with a slice of star fruit. Arrange decoratively on a platter and serve.

Pumpkin Pie Blintzes

price $16   servings   8   price per serving $2

We like to think of these blintzes as updated mini pumpkin pies. They retain the classic pumpkin pie flavors, but the packaging is much cuter and more manageable. They're perfect for trucking to potlucks and other parties in the fall, and our friends go crazy over the concept and tasty pumpkin filling.

BATTER:

1¼ cups milk

2 eggs

2 tablespoons butter, melted

1 cup flour

Pinch salt

FILLING:

1 (15-ounce) can pumpkin

⅓ cup maple syrup

¼ cup sweetened condensed milk

3 tablespoons cinnamon, plus extra for topping

2 tablespoons nutmeg

4 tablespoons butter (½ stick), melted

Powdered sugar, for topping

For batter, whisk ingredients together in large bowl until smooth. Heat large nonstick pan to medium-high heat. Using ½ cup dry measuring utensil, scoop batter into pan. Move pan in circular motion so crepe assumes circular shape. Once top of crepe is no longer liquid (about 30 seconds), turn over with spatula; cook another 15 seconds, until light brown. Make crepes in advance and set aside. Stack with paper towels in between so they don't stick together. Preheat oven to 350°F. For filling, combine all ingredients in large bowl; use mixer on medium speed to whip until fluffy. Spoon 2 tablespoons filling onto each crepe; roll up. Place in very lightly greased baking pan; bake 20 minutes. Sprinkle with cinnamon and powdered sugar and serve warm.

    Part III: Desserts

Red Wine-Poached Pears

price $12   servings 4   price per serving $3

*A*lthough we encounter poached pears often at guest's homes during the holiday season, we can't help but love to make them at home as well. The warm cinnamon-infused wine lends the pears an irresistible aroma and flavor we crave on cold nights.

1 bottle red wine
Juice of 1 lemon
½ cup sugar
½ teaspoon cinnamon
4 medium firm Bartlett pears, peeled, halved, and cored

Combine wine, lemon juice, sugar, and cinnamon in large pot; bring to boil. Add pear halves; reduce heat to simmer. Cover and cook 15–20 minutes, until pears are soft. Remove pears with slotted spoon; set aside to cool. Bring sauce back to boil; reduce by ½, cooking about 10 minutes. Allow sauce to cool; pour over pears. Serve warm with vanilla ice cream, or cool pears 1 hour in refrigerator before serving.

Vanilla Flan

price $12   servings 6   price per serving $2

This recipe is a culinary magic trick. The finished product is extremely impressive, but the process is simple beyond belief. We recommend caramelizing the sugar until it is a deep, dark brown for a sauce that infuses the entire dessert with a deliciously rich and complex flavor.

½ cup sugar

12 extra-large egg yolks

2 (12-ounce) cans evaporated milk

1 (14-ounce) can sweetened condensed milk

1 teaspoon vanilla extract

Preheat oven to 375°F. In small saucepan, melt sugar over medium heat until crystals dissolve and sugar caramelizes to deep brown color. Divide caramelized sugar equally between 2 (8") loaf pans. In large bowl, whisk together yolks, evaporated milk, sweetened condensed milk, and vanilla. Divide mixture equally over caramelized sugar. Cover each pan tightly with foil; place into large baking pan filled with 1" water. Bake 1 hour, or until knife comes out clean. Allow to cool in refrigerator at least 1 hour before serving.

PART III: DESSERTS

DRiNKS

Bloody Mary

price $4   servings 1   price per serving $4

Since this book features so many tasty brunch dishes, we would be disappointed if we couldn't present a beverage to accompany them. This version of the Bloody Mary is heavy on spice and vegetables, but you tone down the seasoning for a milder version.

1 cup tomato juice

Juice of ½ lemon

Dash celery salt

4 dashes Worcestershire sauce

1 teaspoon fresh basil, chopped

1 ounce vodka

¼ teaspoon horseradish

Dash ground black pepper

Dash Tabasco sauce

Celery stalk (for garnish)

Combine all ingredients except celery stalk in shaker; shake vigorously 30 seconds. Pour over ice into highball glass. Garnish with celery stalk and serve.

Spiked Shirley Temple

price $2   servings 1   price per serving $2

These adult-version Shirley Temples are frivolous, girly, and utterly delicious. We love that they're hot pink and garnished with a cherry, and we serve them as a staple beverage at many of our parties.

½ ounce grenadine

2 ounces vodka

4 ounces lemon-lime soda

Maraschino cherry for garnish

In a highball glass, combine grenadine and vodka. Fill glass with ice; top off with lemon-lime soda. Garnish with cherry.

Fruity Smoothies

price $18   servings 4   price per serving $4.50

*T*hese smoothies are low-cal but have enough sweetness for a satisfying dessert. Making smoothies is more art than science, so don't worry about exact measurements.

2 cups frozen strawberries	1 cup vanilla yogurt
1 banana, sliced	½ cup orange juice
1 cup pineapple, kiwi, or frozen blueberries	3 tablespoons honey
5 ice cubes	

Put fruit, ice, and yogurt in blender; pour in juice until it comes about half way up fruit mixture. Add honey; blend until smooth.

Fancy Homemade Hot Cocoa

price $8   servings 4   price per serving $2

*T*his recipe is as easy as microwaving a mug of water and hot cocoa mix, but it tastes infinitely better. Instead of drinking hot water filled with grainy chocolate bits, you'll be sipping a smooth concoction of warm, thick chocolate, sweetened to your taste. You can even experiment with different types of chocolate or adding other flavorings and liqueurs like almond or hazelnut.

2 cups milk	⅓ cup sugar, or more, to taste
3 ounces bitter chocolate, chopped, plus a bit extra for shavings	Whipped cream

Heat milk on low heat on stove. When sufficiently hot, add chopped chocolate; stir into milk. Stir in sugar; remove from heat. Top with whipped cream and chocolate shavings.

Grownup Hot Chocolate

price $10   servings 2   price per serving $5

*O*ne of our first dates was over this hot chocolate. Alex had come into a bottle of brandy, and as college sophomores, we couldn't think of better use for the stuff than turning it into hot chocolate. Simmering the chocolate and alcohol together allows the flavors to gently meld together and results in a grownup treat with darker, more complex flavors than your average hot chocolate.

> 4 ounces dark chocolate (about ½ cup chopped)
> 2 cups milk
> ½ cup sugar
> 1 ounce coffee liqueur
> 1 ounce brandy
> Whipped cream (optional)

In small bowl, melt chocolate in microwave or over a double boiler. In small saucepan, combine milk and sugar; bring to gentle simmer. Add melted chocolate; whisk until fully incorporated. Add coffee liqueur and brandy. Serve warm with whipped cream.

Mint Limeade Spritzer

price $9   servings 6   price per serving $1.50

*D*uring the one summer we spent in the sweltering Philadelphia heat, we would make this refreshing limeade every weekend and have a tall glass after arriving home from work every day. The prospect of this sweetly cooling drink kept us going on even the hottest days.

2 cups water
1¾ cups sugar
⅓ cup coarsely chopped fresh mint
1 cup fresh lime juice
6 cups club soda
Mint (for garnish)

Combine water, sugar, and mint in small saucepan; bring to boil. Cook until sugar dissolves, stirring constantly. Remove from heat; cool in refrigerator 10 minutes. Strain out mint solids through fine sieve. Combine mint syrup and lime juice in pitcher with ice; mix well. Add club soda immediately before serving; pour into tall glasses. Garnish with fresh mint.

Warm Bourbon Apple Cider

price $16   servings 8   price per serving $2

We always buy too much apple cider during the fall and have to make this drink for friends to finish it all. It's a cozy drink for cool fall evenings, and the orange adds an exotic hint of citrus that makes the beverage simply irresistible.

1 tablespoon cloves
1 orange
½ gallon apple cider
¼ cup mulling spices
1 cup bourbon

Stick cloves into orange skin. In large pot, combine apple cider, mulling spices, and clove-studded orange. Gently simmer on medium-low heat 15–20 minutes, until cider is aromatic. Strain out mulling spices and orange. Add bourbon. Pour into mugs and serve warm.

Index

Acknowledgments

It is not possible to express the depth and sincerity of our gratitude toward everyone who helped us write this book. Our families and friends not only encouraged and supported us, but they assumed the enormous responsibility of helping to edit and test 200 recipes. This book would be filled with empty and poorly edited pages if not for their generous ideas, techniques, tips, and inspiration. We are extremely lucky to have such wonderful people in our lives, and we are filled with appreciation and admiration for their efforts.

Firstly, a million thanks go to our meticulous recipe testers for their culinary wisdom and helpful suggestions: Maria, Whitney, Jess, Zai, Sue, Emma, Lilian, Kate, Traci, Liz H., Jon and Katie, Jamie, Melissa, Liz W., Ellen, Patty, the Clarke family, Annette, the Leaman family, Joanne, and Betsy. We are additionally so thankful to everyone who shared family recipes with us and whose brilliant dishes inspired our own: Karen, Jeff, Diane, Rob, Cara, Paula, Amy, Dave, Hannah, Jared and Adina, Cristina, DD, Anita, the Yepes family, and the Campbell family.

We are forever indebted to all of our former roommates, who have not only tolerated our never-ending messes but also often cleaned them up. Sitting down to dinner with you is the reason we love to cook. Thank you to Jacqui, Corissa, Andrew, Ryan, Sadie, Hailey, Steve, and Matt. Danny: You were with us the day we wrote our first blog post and the day we finished this book; the journey would have been way less fun without you.

In addition to those listed above, we are so happy to have friends who have been beyond kind and supportive throughout this process. We owe our sanity to Lara, Mara, mamaflig., KLAWES, section 19 at CLS, David, and Matty.

An extremely heartfelt thanks to Pilar, who plucked our blog from the obscurity of the Internet and convinced us we could become authors. There is no doubt this book would not exist without her. Thanks also to Chelsea, Wendy, and Adams Media, whose belief in this idea has both surprised and motivated us.

A super special thanks goes to Lizzie for her editing, and to Michael, Jonathan, and Phil.

Finally, we thank our parents. As if they hadn't done enough for this book by teaching us to cook, giving us free reign of their kitchens, testing our dishes, funding countless meals, and sharing all of their recipes, they also edited every single page of it. Their aid, support, and love have been more than invaluable. We are the luckiest kids on the planet to have you, and, as you know, this book is yours in more ways than one.

About the Authors

Alanna Kaufman

Alanna Kaufman is originally from Bethesda, Maryland. She has always loved writing, and she served as city news editor of the *Daily Pennsylvanian* while attending the University of Pennsylvania with Alex. She also spent a year writing for Slashfood, AOL's food blog. In addition to writing for Two Fat Als, Alanna is attending Columbia Law School in New York City.

Alex Small

Alex grew up in Easton, Connecticut, where he began experimenting in the kitchen at an early age. He met Alanna at the University of Pennsylvania in 2005, while serving as a senior photography editor at the *Daily Pennsylvanian*. In 2006, the pair created the popular food blog, Two Fat Als, for which Alex manages the web design and photography. He is currently living in New York City, attending Mount Sinai School of Medicine.